In The
Name Of
Jaysus!

 Colin Murphy is the co-author of eighteen other Feckin' books, as well as an acclaimed Irish historical novel, *Boycott*, and two non-fiction books. His last book, *Who's Feckin' Who in Irish History?*, was shortlisted for the prestigious Paddy Power Political Book Awards in London. His pastimes include hillwalking, swimming, visiting the pub and griping about all the stuff we in Ireland seem to do arseways, and, as there is so much of this, he obviously has to visit the pub frequently. He is married to Gráinne and they have two adult kids, Emmet and Ciára.

 Brendan O'Reilly is an illustrator and senior art director in the world of advertising. When not working, he likes to relax by moaning and complaining about the state of the country over a pint or five. When he's not in the pub, he can be found in the hills; he is the first person to climb every mountain in Ireland over 500 metres, despite being as old as the hills himself. He is married to Bernie, and they have two children, Vincent and Isobel.

IN THE NAME OF JAYSUS!

STUFF THAT DRIVES IRISH PEOPLE ROUND THE FECKIN' BEND

COLIN MURPHY &
BRENDAN O'REILLY

THE O'BRIEN PRESS
DUBLIN

First published 2015 by The O'Brien Press Ltd
12 Terenure Road East, Rathgar, Dublin 6, D06 HD27, Ireland.
Tel: +353 1 4923333; Fax: +353 1 4922777
E-mail: books@obrien.ie
Website: www.obrien.ie

ISBN: 978-1-84717-771-1

1 3 5 7 8 6 4 2
15 17 19 20 18 16

Printed and bound in Poland by Białostockie Zakłady Graficzne S.A.
The paper in this book is produced using pulp from managed forests.

THIS BOOK IS DEDICATED TO ALL
THE PEOPLE WHO REFUSE TO ACCEPT
THE BULLSHIT WE HAVE TO PUT UP WITH IN IRELAND.

CONTENTS

1 Shop chains that charge more in Ireland than in Britain

You know the score. You've been there. We all have. You pick up a shirt or a pair of knickers in a shop and, like most people, the first thing you look at is the price tag. In Ireland, price tags often have two prices marked on them, one in euro and the other in sterling. You can see that the item is, say, €20. So far so good. But then you notice that the sterling price is £12. Of course, at the moment, if you exchange €20 you should expect roughly £16, so why, in the name of Jaysus, do our British friends pay £4 less than us miserable eejits?

And it doesn't stop at clothes. Supermarkets are masters at the art of separating us Irish from our spondulicks – for them, it's like shooting fish in a barrel. Almost every item here is dearer than in its British equivalent. A survey in 2014 revealed that lots of items were up to 50% dearer here and one veggie – broccoli – was 200% dearer than across the water! Surely the broccoli here is some special variety that will turn you into a sexual titan or an Irish Einstein? No, 'fraid not. It's plain old common or garden broccoli.

Then there are little things like cars, which also cost more here, naturally. And TV services. Books. DVDs. Magazines. Picture frames. Toys (including the adult ones). Carpets. Electrical goods. Computers. Cameras. The list is endless.

And the reason for the price differences between Ireland and the UK? Often when you ask, retailers are suddenly as scarce as shite from a rocking horse. But, when one of them does come up with an explanation, it's usually some oul' guff about 'overheads being higher here'. What a load of oul' bollix! Is that really why it costs, say, 30% more for a pair of socks in Drogheda than in Newry, a stone's throw away? Or why it costs 20% more to send a satellite signal into your house than to one in Bristol? Go and ask me arse!

The real reason is known to retailers as 'The Paddy Premium'. They charge what they think the market will bear. In other words, they know they can make a gansey-load of free extra cash simply by charging us poor eejits more, as they also know that our legislators aren't going to do anything about it because they're about as useful a concrete currach. Water and property taxes are bad enough, but effectively being taxed for being Irish is enough to drive you to drink. Oh, hang on – that's dearer here as well!

Now remember, forget the jewels and go for the broccoli.

2 Brutal Motorway/Roadside Sculptures

You've probably driven past them a thousand times. But every time you pass one at 120km/hour, this thought briefly flicks through your head: *What the f*** is that wojus yoke?* You then continue on your journey, the lump of twisted metal you just passed already fading from memory. Until that is you pass it again going in the other direction, when the thought once again occurs: *No, really, what the f*** is that wojus yoke?*

What it is, is a piece of public art funded from the Percentage Arts Scheme, which means that a small fraction of any publicly funded project must be allocated to the commissioning of a work of art. That all sounds very admirable, as we're all keen on supporting the arts and struggling artists and so on. The problem arises when it comes to the question of what local country councillors believe constitutes a work of art, as opposed to a big lump of ganky shite. Very often they seem unable to distinguish between the two.

Of course all of art is subjective – one man's masterpiece is another's piece of codology. So with that in mind, let's explore a few examples of the art works that have so illuminated

commuters' lives.

Let's start with the yokes on the M7 Kildare town bypass, which resemble a bunch of ginormous plastic children's windmills. Officially, 'the configuration recreates the feel of the rails around the nearby racecourse'. Well, of course, you knew that, didn't you?

Hopping across to the N2 near Ashbourne in Meath, we meet the giant rusty origami rabbit. Well, that makes perfect sense, origami being such a traditional art form in Ireland.

Very appropriately, Mayo County Council chose some humongous bent metal pipes to represent hot air rising (most of it presumably in the council chamber), for their art installation on the Station Road in Castlebar.

Gorey Bypass in Wexford has been graced by what the locals call the 'rusty stegosaurus'. Actually it's a giant hedgehog. Glad that's cleared up because, with the country broke, you'll appreciate that a giant rusty hedgehog is exactly the sort of thing we desperately need.

Carlow County Council has chosen to enhance our humdrum lives by putting an immense sculpture of a pair of concrete welly boots near Leighlinbridge. Oops, sorry, they actually depict the thrones of the ancient kings of Leinster. Obvious when you think about it.

Rust seems to be the 'in' thing these days. The N21 in Kerry boasts a giant rusty head-the-ball with his arms outstretched, upon which are perched six birds. This is inspired by the Songs of Amergin, a mythical Celtic poet, we're told officially, just in case we couldn't have worked that out for ourselves.

You may have spotted the six wonky telegraph poles sticking out of the ground near the M4/M6 junction. Each has a sort of disc stuck on top. No, they're not some banjaxed communications experiment, but represent figures from our ancient past on a journey towards awareness, collecting knowledge as they travel. Just the way *you're* travelling, and *you're* being enlightened by art. Geddit?

Thanks to our county councillors being so in touch with their inner artistic muses, we have been gifted with gazillions of inspirational pieces all over the country. But pride of place has to go to the giant piece of sh…sculpture near Ballindine,

County Mayo. This 10m-high multi-coloured masterpiece represents an accordion, and celebrates the work of a local musician, Martin O'Donoghue. For the benefit of those yet to feast their eyes on the work, it essentially resembles a gargantuan steel jaw-trap stood on its side, the teeth being bright red and yellow and the rest bright blue. To get a sense of its scale, the hole in the middle could easily accommodate a zeppelin.

Jaysus, they must have really hated that poor oul' fecker Martin's guts.

Apparently it represents pre-Christian Brehon society expressed through the contents of a skip.

3 FOREIGNERS WHO THINK WE ARE PART OF BRITAIN

You're sure to have met one or two of these saps. Despite decades of global TV coverage about the North, and despite virtually every westernised country having a ginormous Irish population, you still get the occasional eejit who thinks we're Brits. And the sad fact is, that there is still a sizeable number of Brits who think we're Brits!

There you are on holiday in Disneyland, queuing up to get into Buzz Lightyear's Astro Blasters, when this guy next to you hears your accent and asks in a friendly way where you hail from. 'Ireland', you reply proudly, only to get a response something like, 'Oh yeah, my wife loves your Queen Elizabeth.' Before he's even finished his sentence, you're looking around for a large Mickey Mouse statue to insert into his arse. But unfortunately, our American friends aren't the only guilty parties. The French, Germans, Italians, Spanish etc. can display equal levels of pig ignorance.

To be fair, it can be a bit confusing for the foreign lads. See, we're an independent republic, but a bit of the island is part of the UK, but not part of Britain. Also, we're part of 'the

British Isles', which is a purely geographical term meaning the two islands of Britain and Ireland. And then our rugby team represents the whole island, yet we have two soccer teams. Add to that, in the Olympics it's Britain, but in the World Cup, it's England, Scotland, Wales, N. Ireland and the Republic of Ireland. Yet all we want is for foreign feckers to remember that, politically, we have zilch, zero, nada to do with Britain!

A few years ago an Aussie commentator called Russel Barwick made the error of saying it was an Irish joke that Ireland wasn't part of the British Olympic team, especially as we were part of the 'British Lions' rugby team. Actually we play as part of the 'British and Irish Lions' rugby team, but the gobshite was too dense to even know that. He then went on to say: 'I understand the history of Irish politics. Well. . . I don't understand the history of Irish politics.' Well, duh. After about 20 million outraged Irish called him everything from a wojus gouger to an ignorant Aussie bollix, poor Russell got the message.

The Irish don't mind a bit of slagging, and you can pretty much call us anything without offending us. Just don't call us Brits.

Bartender, how far is it from Dublin to Loch Ness?

4 THE BAN ON ALCOHOL SALES ON GOOD FRIDAY

You know, it's amazing the number of Irish people who suddenly develop an interest in Irish theatre on Good Friday and take themselves off to see Ibsen's *Hedda Gabler* or Synge's *Deirdre of the Sorrows*. Why this annual upsurge in interest in our great literary tradition? Simple, a licensed theatre is one of the only places you can enjoy a few scoops on Good Friday. So all over the country you have semi-pissed eejits looking at actors

Good Friday in Ireland

on stage and muttering, 'What de f**k's dis bleedin' ting about?'

Yes, we are quite unique in our almost-ban on alcohol sales on Good Friday, which dates from a 1927 law that also prohibited getting rat-arsed on Christmas Day and St Patrick's Day. Yes, you read that right. Now known as the world's biggest booze-fest, the law banning alcohol on Paddy's Day was only rescinded in 1960 as it was decided this was not good for tourism, and nobody kicked up a fuss. Of course, Good Friday was different, it having such special significance in the global Catholic Church. The imbibing of alcohol on Good Friday was deemed by our local clerical hierarchy as a fierce bad mortal sin.

One of the gas side-effects of the ban is known as the Holy Thursday Stampede. You can observe this in any supermarket where you'll see queues of head-the-balls with trolleys crammed with trays of beer, multi-packs of wine and litres of spirits. Of course, the amount purchased far exceeds the amount of alcohol that anyone could safely consume in a day, but the thought of the next-day's drought seems to induce a form of mass neurosis that can only be alleviated by the knowledge that there's enough booze in the house to kill a herd of elephants.

Then there's the famous Last Orders Ritual on Holy Thursday. No sooner do the pub lights flicker than there are hundreds of people screaming orders for eight pints – and that's just for the missus.

Despite the fact that the church has lost most of its influence in government circles, the ban remains. It's like all those TDs are still secretly scared to bejaysus that if they suggest rescinding it, they'll be burnt at the stake or something.

Luckily there are numerous ways of getting around the ban.

The first, already mentioned, is to attend the theatre or another national cultural institution.

Then there's the train, plane or boat journey. Just buy a ticket to somewhere over 40km away and you can get happily fluthered on the vehicle, or if you can't be arsed travelling, simply stay in the station/terminal bar. It's like a holy ticket really – it's as though it buys a special dispensation from sin.

Another way is at a horse or greyhound race meeting. You see, gambling on this most special holy day is not deemed sinful and, within the confines of the racetrack, neither is getting gee-eyed.

'The 8.30 express to complete inebriation is now leaving platform 3'.

There's the option of walking across the border into Northern Ireland where you can imbibe to your heart's content, but this be a problem for people living in say, west Cork.

And lastly, you could check into a hotel. You see in the old days it was assumed that hotel guests were generally foreign heathens, and who cared if those dirty gougers burnt in hell?

Just one question – if it is so sinful to drink alcohol on Good Friday, how come you can have a beer in the Vatican café?

5 PEOPLE MOANING ABOUT THE HEAT WHEN WE HAVE A COUPLE OF DAYS' SUNSHINE

Living in Ireland you tend to hear the phrase 'Isn't the weather bleedin' desperate?' quite often, given that it's lashing every other day. Fair enough, you say. You can understand people moaning about regularly getting so soaked you could wring them out like a sponge. What's *not* fair enough, though, are gobshites who start whingeing when we have our three or four annual days of sunshine during the 'summer'.

Yes, only in Ireland can we moan about any good fortune that might come our way. But you can rest assured that when the thermometer sky-rockets to something like, say, 19°C,

Wouldn't you love a bit of freezing fog?

Or a nice shower of sleet?

people all over the country will be walking around wiping their foreheads, puffing their cheeks and declaring, 'Jaysus, I'm feckin' swelterin'. Gimme a bit of grey skies any day.' You can also be sure that when the dark clouds do arrive the next day, the same head-the-balls will be heard moaning to the high heavens that they've 'a pain in the hole with the weather here', and that they're 'off to Fuerteventura for a bit o' sun'.

Then you have the dopes who whinge that their gardens are dying for a drop of rain. This in a country where Noah could build an ark every March confident it would be afloat by September. To those worried about their 'parched plants' – don't. Really. More rain is on the way.

And then there are the whingers who go on endlessly about 'not knowing what to wear', given our changeable climate. Well, boo-hoo. Deal with it, you big eejits. One thing is certain, you're not going to have the problem for long.

...And I'm afraid the unrelenting sunshine is set to continue...

6 THE NCT FAILING YOUR CAR FOR SOMETHING PATHETIC

Your car is in perfect condition. Tyres. Brakes. Steering. Light alignment. Bodywork. Brake lights. Nothing to worry about at the National Car Testing centre *this* time. OK, it was a pain in the arse having to give up half a day's holiday to have the thing checked out, but at least you're going to be in the clear for a couple of years.

Then the guy calls you over to his stupid little window.

'Fail.'

'What?!!! Why?!!!!! Are you actin' the bleedin' maggot?'

With a smug grin, he explains himself. Apparently the

manufacturer of your car put a trendy extra brake light in the rear window of your banger, and it's banjaxed. So, even though your standard brake lights are hunkydory and your car is perfectly safe, this eejit fails you because a light that you don't need – and probably didn't even know was there – is kaput. The guy sends you out into the streets raging like a bull with its arse on fire, your brain concocting plots to return some dark night and blow the entire NCT building to smithereens in revenge.

Then there's the ever-popular light alignment. Ever-popular with the geebag NCT technicians, that is. Now, aligning your lights involves twiddling a little knob in most cars, but of course nobody knows how much to twiddle up or down to get

Sorry, Ma'am. Chewing gum in the ashtray...

the beams right. Fail. You didn't twiddle up enough. Or down enough. Who knows?

Condensation on the inside of a light housing? Fail!

Airbag indicator light not working? Fail!

A 1cm crack in foglight cover? Fail!

Rear seatbelt buckle shoved down behind seat? Fail!

Wrong font on reg. plate? Fail!

Indicator light not amber enough? Fail!

All of the above are genuine reasons people's cars have failed. And each one of these, of course, costs you money and time to repair, before you can book a re-test, which costs you more money and time. What a bunch of shitehawks!

Why does the word 'scam' pop into mind?

NCT system? Fail.

7 MEANINGLESS ELECTRONIC SIGNS AT BUS STOPS

Isn't it great to see that our national transport companies are moving with the times? Long gone are the days when we had a paper book of timetables that were utterly meaningless. Now we have expensive, state-of-the-art digital signs at every bus stop that are utterly meaningless.

The old book was comparable to *Ulysses,* in that it was a complete work of fiction and a perusal of its pages would leave you scratching your head – but at least it was good for lighting a fire or swatting a fly. The new system, on the other hand, serves no purpose other than to act as a conversation starter for the masses of frustrated commuters waiting at bus stops in our cities where these signs exist.

Example – your fictional bus, let's call it the 17A (oops, sorry, that's not a fictional bus, although that's debatable). Ok, let's call it √-1 (or the square root of minus one, as we all know). So, your √-1 is due in '15 min', says the trendy sign. After five minutes, it naturally changes to '10 min.' Then to '5 min', '4 min,' '3 min,' and '2 min.' Your heart begins to pound in expectation. Finally you can escape the biting wind and rain and the girl with wojus BO standing next to you. The sign announces '1 min'. You look along the road in expectation of that beautiful number √-1 bus.

Nothing happens. You wait a minute or two. Nothing happens. Then the sign changes back to '5 min.' Then to '7 min.' Then the shaggin' thing disappears altogether! It is as though somewhere along the route an alien spaceship has beamed the number √-1 bus into space. Or perhaps it never existed in the first place, and they were just messin' with your head for fun.

Meanwhile, back at the bus stop, the gnashing of teeth has drowned out the sound of the howling, icy gale.

Perhaps our national bus companies should renumber all their buses √-1, √-2, √-3, and so on, as like many of the buses themselves, they're all numbers that simply don't exist.

8 Ringing the Public Service

Ring. Ring.

(Automated answering service.) 'Hello, you've reached the Department of Dossers. Please select the service you require. If you want Form 2469A, press 1. If you want your local branch of useless eejits, press 2. If you want a talk to an expert on wasting taxpayers' hard-earned cash, press 3. If you would like to waste your precious time by speaking to a public servant, press 4 and stay on the line'.

Beep.

'All of our operators are busy, right now. You are currently number (beep) three hundred ... and sixty ... seven ... in line. Here's some really ganky music to annoy you while you wait, which will hopefully give you such a pain in the hole you'll hang up and go away'.

('The Hucklebuck', played on a crap electronic organ, commences, and plays for five minutes.)

'All of our operators are busy right now. You are

currently number (beep) three hundred ... and sixty ... six ... in line. To learn more about our online service visit www. wojuswebsitethatdoesn'twork.ie'.

(Music resumes for a further five minutes.)

'All of our operators are busy, right now. You are currently number (beep) three hundred ... and sixty ... five ... in line. If you would like to learn more about why the public service should have a massive pay hike without improving our performance by as much as a gnat's gonad, then you need to see a shrink'.

(Music resumes for a further five minutes.)

'All of our operators are busy, right now. You are currently (beep) three hundred ... and sixty ... four ... in line. If you would....'

Beep. (Line goes dead.)

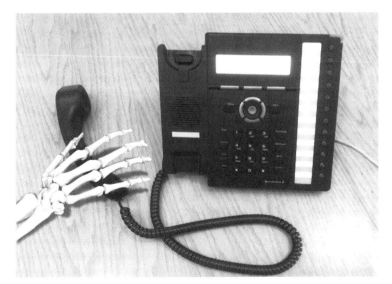

9 WHY DOES A GLASS OF BEER NOT COST HALF THE PRICE OF A PINT OF BEER?

You're out for a nice relaxing drink with the missus or the hubby and you go up to the bar and order a pint and a glass of Guinness (a glass, for overseas readers, being a uniquely Irish term for a half-pint). The cost of a pint varies enormously across the country, as we know, and can go from €3.50 to €6, depending on where you are (except in the case of the Temple Bar quarter of Dublin, where they charge a tenner just to allow you lick the dregs from a dirty glass).

But for the sake of argument, let's say the pint of Guinness costs €4.50. Naturally, your bill should total €6.75, i.e. the price of a pint added to the price of a half-pint. Simple mathematics. Any five-year-old could work it out. Of course, the publican universe is a very strange place where the ordinary laws of

Half-pint, Spock? **That would be illogical, Captain.**

mathematics don't apply. Which is why you are presented with a bill for €7.75. Huh? Let me see, a pint cost €4.50 but a half-pint costs €3.25?

What's the story, Rory? Well, you see, the official excuse is that pulling two half-pints as opposed to one pint requires extra labour, which accounts for the higher cost. So to take our example, the act of lifting or washing two separate glasses, something that requires about as much effort as scratching your left buttock, is charged at a rate of €1 per mammoth effort. Were you to apply that rate to other walks of life, a part-time trolley collector in a supermarket would annually earn about the same as a major international oil conglomerate.

Let's hope other industries don't try to get in on this uniquely Irish rip-off. Imagine if the same ganky logic applied when buying steak or cheese or crisps or petrol or onions or land or chairs or carpet or any f***ing thing on the planet, for that matter!

In the meantime, Irish vintners are forever whingeing about the raw deal they get. What a bunch of hypocritical gougers.

Pint and a glass.

10 IRISH PEOPLE USING BRITISH-SPEAK

A few years ago a gift card company conducted a poll for Mother's Day asking Irish people what they called their mothers. The vast majority used 'Mam', followed by 'Ma', and trailing way behind in third place was 'Mum' (mostly from D4).

Yet you'd never guess this from all the gobdaw wannabe Brits on our TV and radio stations. Almost universally, they have decided to impose 'Mum' on us, presumably as they think it makes them sound British, and therefore, superior to us ordinary Irish Joe Soaps. Of course, anyone is entitled to call their mother whatever they want, including 'ye manky oul' wagon', but the thing is, that the vast majority of these media 'celebrities' call their mother 'Mam' in private, but use 'Mum'

Can I fondle your thrupenny bits, Philomena?

Seamus, don't you ever think of anything but Posh 'n' Becks?

Oi, Guv'nor! Bung us some dosh for the dog and bone.

when broadcasting. So, as your Irish Mams or Mas would have said, the gougers should go and feck off with themselves.

Unfortunately, this Brit-speak that is creeping into Ireland is not limited to 'celebrities'. Thanks, of course, to our nation being force-fed British soaps and shows, such as the seriously wojus *X-Factor*, it is becoming more common to hear people use words and phrases like 'ball & chain', 'plonker', 'jimmy riddle', 'chin wag' and 'a cuppa cha'. There's even a café in Dublin that sells 'bangers' as part of the full Irish breakfast. Yeuch, in every sense.

The worst offenders of all are those who have begun to address Irish males as 'mate'. It's an almost daily occurrence now. Of course there's nothing wrong with a British man addressing his friend as 'mate'. It's a free world. But, you see, we're not British. We're Irish. And most of us are proud of that fact. And our forefathers fought and died to make that a reality. So can there possibly be anything more ganky, false, grating and insincere that an Irishman calling a fellow Irishman 'mate', just so he can sound like a Brit?

If so addressed, respond thus: 'I'm not your 'mate'. I've never seen ye before in me life, ye big ignorant gobshite! Go an' ask me bollix, and, while you're at it, shove your "mate" up your feckin' arse.'

That's tellin' 'em. Innit, bruv?

11 PEOPLE WHO ARE STUCK IN A CIVIL WAR MENTALITY

In virtually every country in Europe the political divide is left and right of centre, with a few liberals, greens and independents thrown into the mix. Not here, of course. That would make too much sense. No, our main political parties have traditionally been divided by an ideology that's as relevant to most people today as a lecture by 1970s agony aunt, Angela Macnamara, about the evils of pre-marital sex.

Well, guys, here's some news for you. The Civil War ended a very, *very* long time ago and, at this stage, nobody gives a shite which side your grandfather fought on.

Yet, hard as it is to believe, there are those gobdaws of relative youth who still get their knickers in a tangle over some obscure point of Civil War codology. A few years ago when Fine Gael invited the late Brian Lenihan, of Fianna Fáil, to speak at the annual Michael Collins commemoration, a large number of absolute mentallers crawled out of the woodwork to take issue, including a Fine Gael senator and a well-known, old blueshirt eejit broadcaster, to mention but a couple. And amazingly, there are those who refuse to vote for one or the other party because they represent the so-called 'republican' or 'free state' sides, particularly in rural Ireland. Does it matter that they're both essentially conservative parties with precisely the same manky policies? You must be bleedin' coddin'. To put this in context, it's a bit like Austrians and Bosnians still hating each others' guts over the assassination of Archduke Franz feckin' Ferdinand in 1914.

Tell you what, lads. Why don't you diehard Civil War saps get together in Croker and kick the crap out of each other, while the rest of us do something of real importance, like not give a shite.

12 Road signs that make absolutely no sense

It is a regular occurrence in Ireland to pull off a dual carriageway or primary national road, where the speed limit was probably 100km/hr, and then in the blink of an eye find yourself on a seriously minor country lane with grass growing down the middle and brambles scratching either side of your car – and where the speed limit is 80-, 90- or even 100km/hr! Frankly, to drive at anything like 80km/hr on one of these 'roads' is about as easy as a one-legged man winning an arse-

Dursey Island, Co. Cork. Yes, really.

kicking contest. Yet you can bet your house there are plenty of morons out there willing to try – and, sure, why wouldn't they, as their homicidal rally-cross speeding has been sanctioned by the Department of Transport?

Seriously. How in Holy Mary, Mother of God's name did someone decide that a boreen barely wide enough to fit a skinny oul' lad on a bike, and covered with weeds and cowshite, is fit for a car travelling at high speed? When you think about it, someone had to dig a hole, fill it with cement, put a metal pole in it and fix a sign to the top, so it's not like it was thrown up in a couple of minutes. Didn't it occur to ANYONE that such a speed limit was completely arseways? Or maybe, on discovering that they had no 30-, 40-, or 50km signs, they just used what they had on the back of the truck, as they just didn't give a flying feck – sure who's going to say anything? Nobody in the Department of Transport gives a shite either!

And there are lots of other examples of road signs that make no sense. Take this sign: Sligo 179km; five kilometres later: Sligo 182km. Another common occurrence. Either someone couldn't be arsed driving 10km further to put the sign in the right place, or some Einsteinian distortion in the time-space continuum has just occurred.

The first line in the Wikipedia entry on road signs in Ireland states that 'Road signs in Ireland mostly differ from traffic signs elsewhere in Europe'.

Go on! Really? Oh, and by the way, the Pope's a Catholic.

13 After Years of Grinding Austerity, Setting Up a Water Company With a Bonus Culture

Here's an imaginary cabinet meeting from a few years back:

Enda: Right guys. The troika are gone. The property tax is up and running. Now we'll have to come up with a new way to really piss the people off. Something that'll get them out on the streets and have them screaming for our heads.

Phil: Water! What about taxing water?

Enda: Good one, Phil. That would really be a pain in the arse for everyone. (Scratches his forehead.) But I'm not sure it would be enough. Sure, haven't we hit the poor bastards with all sorts

No tap water, thank you. We'll just have plain old bottled.

41

of taxes?

James: How about we hire a shower of thicks to run this new water company, who don't know their arse from their elbow about water, and pay them gansey-loads of money?

Enda: I like your thinking, James. Similar to your Department of Health policy.

James: Exactly.

Eamon: I'd like to make a suggestion. Speaking as a socialist, it would really get on everyone's tits if the new company then hired a bunch of consultants at vastly excessive rates to tell them sweet f-all.

Enda: And who said the coalition isn't a team, Eamon!

Joan: Taoiseach! I just thought! As a woman of the people, I can tell you that the one thing that is absolutely guaranteed to make everyone as mad as a bull with a beehive up its arse, is if the new water company has a bonus culture!

Enda: Ah, Joan, you're a woman after me own heart. With thinking like that, you'll be leader of the Labour Party one day! That's it! It was bad enough that we let all the Celtic Tiger criminal gougers get off scot-free, but what really drove the people of Ireland round the bend was the bonus culture in all those banjaxed banks and State institutions. But they think that's all in the past. They think the days of getting a bonus for being a bowsie that's brutal at your job are over. (Rubs his hands together.) Well, we'll show the feckin' people that it's not! We'll show the poor bastards that we're as big a bunch of cute hoors as Fianna Fáil! Over to you, Phil!

14 The Angelus

Imagine if you lived in Northern Ireland and every day at, say, 5pm, an Orange Order pipe band blared out 'The Protestant Boys' on the national broadcaster's TV and radio channels in honour of the moment King Billy declared victory over James II at the Battle of the Boyne? You can envisage what the rest of Ireland – hang on – the rest of the civilised world would make of that! There would be cries of sectarianism, discrimination, bigotry etc. And rightly so. Luckily, our friends in the north aren't such a bunch of geebags.

Have you ever heard of the Angelus?

Doesn't ring any bells.

Unlike us, that is, or to put it more accurately, unlike the head-the-balls who run RTÉ and who haven't the *liathroidí* to put an end to the twice-daily bong-bong-bong of the Angelus – a sectarian statement that we're a country where Catholics run the gaff, thanks very much, and all you Prods, Muslims, Jews, Hindus, Buddhists and worshippers of the Great God Mumbi Gangibum can go and feck off with yourselves.

Apparently, it was that looper, Archbishop John Charles McQuaid, who came up with the idea of broadcasting the Angelus in 1949. Of course nowadays Ireland is a multi-ethnic, multi-denominational country. People now worship Vishnu, Jesus, Allah, Yehovah, property and various football teams. But tell that to the big-shot eejits out in Montrose, who seem to be terrified that McQuaid's heavenly spirit will have a word in God's ear and deny them everlasting happiness if they scrap the slot.

Having said that, even though they're such bunch of scardey sleeveens when it comes to the Angelus, RTÉ as a rule can be proud of the balance it brings in matters of belief. So in the interests of continuing that fine tradition, here's a suggestion: Besides the Angelus, let's have the Islamic call to prayer the traditional five times a day, a Protestant pipe band a couple of times, a few blasts of the shofar to summon our Jewish pals to pray, and a few mantras for the Hindu faithful.

No?

Why not?

Ok, maybe it would be easier to scrap the Angelus.

And we'd even have the bonus of not having to look at all those mentallers on TV staring dreamily into space while it's on, as if they've just had a couple of really great spliffs.

15 THE WAY THE WHOLE COUNTRY GRINDS TO A STANDSTILL WHEN THERE'S A FEW CM OF SNOW

Massive tailbacks in all major Irish cities. People abandoning cars. Bus services cancelled or curtailed. Flights diverted. Ferry sailings cancelled. Huge upsurge in people calling into work sick. Hospitals inundated with admissions.

Is this a movie about an Ebola-like plague sweeping Ireland? Is it a simulation for some future disaster that might strike the country?

No, it is none of these things. It's simply the reality that occurs every winter when Ireland is 'hit' by a couple of centimetres of snow. Yes, when it comes to cold weather, we are definitely the champion wimps of the world.

Met Éireann has taken to issuing weather warnings of late. Now, you'd normally expect that, when a meteorological service issues a warning, some potentially catastrophic weather event is in the offing. Not in Ireland. A recent weather alert was issued that there was the 'threat' of three centimetres of snow across the country. Three bleedin' centimetres! That would barely come above the soles of your shoes! Of course, panic hits the streets. The snow is the main item on the Six O'Clock News. Traffic grinds to a halt. Public transport services collapse. The various councils say that they haven't enough salt to keep the roads clear. People take to their beds en masse as though struck by a deadly epidemic.

Foreigners used to cold climes watch us with bewilderment, scratching their heads and wondering if there's been a military coup or something, such is the chaos that reigns in the streets. In many other countries, people regularly have to find their car with a stick before digging it out, and then driving to work along roads that have already been cleared before sunrise. Temperatures regularly fall below -30°C. Rivers and lakes become solid blocks of ice – and it happens every year. Should anything remotely like these conditions ever hit Ireland just once, half the population would be wiped out, all commerce would cease and the streets would be deserted.

So the next time we get a light dusting of snow in the middle of winter, please don't react with shock/horror/panic.

In fact, just chill.

The Irish snowman; a short but happy life

16 Finding your wheelie bin 50m from your house

LOST

GREY-BLACK COLOUR
ANSWERS TO THE NAME
OF "WHEELY"

Ok, it's not exactly something that you'd get yourself worked up to 90 about, it wouldn't drive you to drink or anything, but its just another example of the ganky level of services we've come to take as being the norm in our fair land.

The bin lorry arrives and there are three or four guys working the bins. Of course, the driver doesn't stop at every house, but perhaps every tenth house. So the bin guy grabs your bin and wheels it halfway down the street, sticks it onto the machine yoke that empties it, and then shoves the thing up against the nearest wall. Come 8am, there's a great melee in the street as 20 people, already late for work, set off on a desperate search to locate and retrieve their wheelie bin. Unmarked bins are mixed up, heated views exchanged, and occasionally the odd blow as well. It's called Wheelie Rage. All thanks to the lazy bowsies who work for the bin company.

Rubbish workers. How apt.

17 HERITAGE GROUPS DEMANDING THE CONSERVATION OF UGLY, DERELICT RUINS

We all love our nice old buildings. They enrich our cities and towns, they're nice to look at, they give our urban areas character and a sense of history. And it's a terrible shame when one of them becomes derelict. As a rule, most people support heritage and conservation groups when they try to rescue an architecturally worthy structure from demolition or collapse. That's grand.

But then, every now and again, you hear a ginormous fuss about some wojus tumbledown yoke that was ugly when it was thrown up in the first place and hasn't improved with age. And, often, all that's left of the original building are about 50 blocks, three lumps of plaster and the plumbing for a Victorian jacks. Yet the hoo-ha you're likely to hear about the destruction of our heritage would make you think someone was planning to blow up the Four Courts. Again.

Really, aren't there better battles to fight? Like saving our genuine Georgian heritage from dereliction? Or stopping companies from covering our fine city centre buildings with signs that have about as much taste as a slapper's make-up?

Having said all that, Irish architects are generally so brutal that any replacement building they throw up will probably be equally ganky. But that's another storey. Ha ha.

A fine example of a 1960s lean-to timber chicken coop.

18 Bad Imitations of
An Irish Accent

There you are, enjoying your movie on a Saturday night, a riveting, psychological drama that has you engrossed, and then suddenly an Irish character enters the plot and starts saying shite like 'Well, bey de hokey, t'isn't it a grand soft day, me deer? Roight! Let's go te de pub and Oil buy ye a noice point of shtout, begob.'

At this point, you pick up the DVD box to see if the movie you thought was a serious drama is actually a slapstick comedy. No. This guy is supposed to be for real. Unfortunately, by now you're finding it as acutely embarrassing as watching a film of yourself dancing rat-arsed when you were 19 years old.

The list of famous actors, often very good ones, who have tried and failed to master the Irish accent is amazing. Leonardo di Caprio, Brad

Pitt, Tom Cruise, Julia Roberts, Gerard Butler, Sean Connery and many, many more. Really guys, can it be that hard?

Actually, if you take a look at the subject on youtube.com, you'll probably get a clue where all these cringe-inducing begorrah-heads get their training. Various 'voice coaches' give the most hilarious lessons on doing an Irish accent, except the poor gobshites don't actually realise they're hilarious. They advise people to add an 'o' before an 'i' so they can say things like 'oil be foine'. One key tip for mastering an Irish accent is to speak with a 'little bubble at the front of your mouth', whatever in the name of holy sweet shite that means.

And there are lots of these big eejits out there, voice-coaching the stars in Oirish. Hollywood actually sends along American voice coaches when they're shooting a movie in Ireland to teach the locals how to speak with a 'proper' Irish accent! No wonder Brad Pitt, Tom Cruise *et al* sound like banjaxed leprechauns. Lads, as we Irish say in our charming, mellifluous accents: 'Go an' ask me bollix.'

19 Scroungers Living Off the State

First off, this is not some rant about foreigners here on welfare holidays. No, this is a rant about scumbags in general on welfare holidays. And Irish people still represent by far the largest number of dossers in Ireland who are claiming benefits to beat the band, not because they were forced into the situation through unemployment or ill-health or whatever, but because they choose it. And, being dossers by nature, why wouldn't they? Ireland, as a rule, is very generous to dossers.

The thing is, most of these lazy geebags demonstrate such a gift for trawling through the volumes of social service bureaucracy to uncover all the little loopholes and freebies and benefits, that they would undoubtedly be an asset to many a company if they put their skills to better use. Most ordinary citizens wouldn't have a clue where to start when faced with a 36-page form, or couldn't be arsed, thinking it's more trouble than its worth. But not the Irish dosser. Form F*ckit-999 and Form D*sserZ101 and all the rest are the dosser's bread and butter, his or her pot of gold at the end of a day on the sofa, watching 'Judge Judy' and 'Survivor' on their plasma TV.

'I need a new pram because the old one's got a chocolate stain...' 'Ok. Here, fill out Form 35T2-1.'

'Sorry, I can't work because, if I do, I'll lose my free gaff...' 'Perfectly understandable. Here's a wad of notes.'

'I can't work because I've a bad back from carryin' around these seven bleedin' children all day. Oh, and by the way, can I get some new maternity bras? I'm up the duff again...' 'No prob. And here's a pile of cash to buy clothes for the nippers. Don't go spending it on fags, now!'

Just as well the country has so much spare cash to throw around at the moment.

20 Having the worst politicians in the Western world (see also: Parish pump politicians)

What is it about Irish politicians that makes them so invariably woeful? This small country has churned out literary geniuses by the cartload, businesspeople who have excelled in every corner of the world, Nobel prize-winning scientists, world champion sports people, great actors, artists, dancers, architects and bands who have enjoyed global success. But our TDs and senators? Almost without exception, what a bleedin' waste of space.

How can this be? Is there something in the air in Leinster House that makes them so useless? Asbestos in the foundation, perhaps, or pyrite in the walls, or a leaky sewer pipe under the jacks?

No. You have to go back to almost the beginning to find the answer – the founding of Fianna Fáil by Dev and pals and the first time it led a government in 1932. They then remained in power for most of the next 70 years during which time Dev isolated Ireland so much that we might as well have been on the moon. Naturally the place went to shit. No money, no jobs, no

hope. You had two choices if you wanted to get by. One was to leg it to somewhere else, the other was become a buddy of some cute hoor in Fianna Fáil.

Thus the age of the parish pump politician, cronyism and corruption was born in Ireland, and it's never really ended. One of the rare exceptions to the bunch of half-wits and sleeveens who sit in the Dáil, was ironically Fianna Fáil's Sean Lemass, who modernised Ireland in the 1960s and had little time for gombeen men and kowtowing to the Catholic Church. But, other than that, it seems that the culture of favouritism, back seat deals and brown envelopes that germinated in the early days of the State has now become accepted as the norm. In other words politics in Ireland doesn't attract bright people who actually want to do anything to improve the country, but eejits with a bit of blarney who don't know their arse from their elbow and see politics purely as a way of improving their own lot. Any politician who is offended by this assessment can go and ask our collective arses, as one merely has to point to the state of the place if proof be needed.

Please, please let any man or woman, with even the teensiest bit of vision, step forward. Because for the last 90 years, no politician's vision has extended beyond the next election.

21 Racists on the Radio

Ireland seems to have a disproportionate number of these uber-saps, but in reality we probably have just about the same proportion as most western European countries. Its just that here we have a whole bunch of radio stations that are happy to facilitate them.

And on the surface they make great radio. Fellow racist sub-humans can sit at home nodding in agreement with views, such as 'those foreign XXXs are takin' all our jobs and then livin' off the f***kin' dole', while their opponents sit at home and get worked up into a right state about the shite that they're hearing on the airwaves. Listenership figures shoot up and the radio stations rub their hands. Virtually every radio station in the country has one of these phone-in shows, to 'facilitate public debate'.

But it's the late-night shows when the true crazies emerge from the toilet. Here's the kind of 'public debate' you're likely to hear:

Caller 1: 'Dese Poles and Lintinanians are all scroungers an' drug addicts, Mick.

Radio guy: That's a very generalised statement, Jacintha.

Caller 1: General eyes, wha? Listen, Mick, deir teachers didn't even learn dem to speak English proper.

Radio guy: But, really, Jacintha, when you say…

Caller 2: Heee-er you! Leave Jacintha 'lone. She's ony sayin' it like it is. Dese black fellas from Latviland are all lazy f******g c***s. Dat righ', Jacintha?

Radio guy: That's a rather strong statement, Anto.

Caller 1: Buh he's righ'. And dey sell their babies in the streeh an' dey eat dat forin muck.

Caller 2: Hey, Jacintha? You sound like a right ri-ed. Want te meet me for a few scoops an' a Chinky?

Caller 1: Deffo, Anto.

Obviously the 'free speech' on which we pride ourselves is a serious misnomer – because the rest of us have to pay the price of enduring this sort of crap.

22 OTT First Holy Communions

Grown-ups like to tell their kids that when they made their first communion they were given something like a fiver in total, or six shillings and a handful of farthings. So they must be sick with jealousy that the average amount that a child gets nowadays is €591. Jammy little bastards.

Of course, many grown-ups only have themselves to blame, as this is what their kids expect when they witness the lengths that their Mas and Das are prepared to go to in the game of First Holy Communion one-upmanship.

First off, it's the clothes, and here it is definitely the girls who get the best/worst treatment (depending on one's personal level of taste(lessness).) At one end of the scale, you have the little girls who appear to be dressed in a conical lump of fancy white icing, and wouldn't be out of place standing on top of a giant cake. Then there are those who have been dressed to resemble a fancy light shade that you'd see dangling from a ceiling. But worst of all are the girls who seem to have been dropped bodily into a giant clump of pink candyfloss, with only their little heads protruding from the top, bearing a tacky tiara studded with fake jewels in myriad colours. Generally, the boys get off easily in terms of (lack of) sartorial elegance, but, at worst, they may have tails and a top hat imposed upon them by their parents.

For any self-disrespecting eejit parent, fake tans are also *de rigueur* nowadays. Not to mention hair-dos that make it appear as though there is a dead squirrel on their child's head.

There is often a brief nod to the religious aspect of First Communions, with the addition to the outfit of holy medals and rosettes, but these are only permissible if they don't clash with the fashion statement, the statement being, 'I have as much taste as a pair of edible jocks.'

Then there's the transport aspect. Stretch limos are the norm. But many have tried to stretch tastelessness beyond even the stretch limo by hiring a horse-drawn carriage. And there are even reports of children arriving in the church grounds by

Guard, I've just been mugged by a small girl in a communion dress.

chopper. Holy Christ.

Next up, is the inconvenient religious ceremony, i.e. 'Will dis bleedin' ting ever end?' After which, all adjourn to a nearby restaurant/pub to get pissed and have a slice from the crucifix-shaped cake. And while the Ma and Da are getting slowly rat-arsed, the kids are outside rolling on the grass in their €500 dresses/suits.

Finally, rounds must be done of aunts, uncles and friends to see how much dosh can be wrung out of them, the aforesaid aunts and uncles knowing full well that their contribution (or lack of it) will be the subject of debate and comparison among the wider family for years to come. So they almost always err on the side of caution and hand over €50 plus.

All of which begs the question – shouldn't it be renamed the First Holy *Collection?*

23 CRAP IRISH TRADESMEN/WOMEN

If you're an Irish tradesman, before steam starts billowing from various orifices, please note that the heading does not read 'All Irish tradesmen/women are crap', but refers only to the substantial number who are, in fact, crap. Actually, 'crap' is doing these feckers a service. 'Wojus' or 'ganky' would probably be more apt.

What's really put the spotlight on these incompetent dossers in the last couple of decades has been the influx of tradespeople from eastern Europe. Of course, not all of these are wonderful either, but the percentages of wojus v good is reversed – and

It seems it's the only tool he doesn't know how to use.

not in the Irish guys' favour. Until the fellas with the accents arrived, everyone in Ireland thought that a lump of plaster hitting you on the head three weeks after the guy 'fixed your ceiling' was the norm. 'Ah, sure what can you do?' we'd say, shaking our noggins as blood streamed down our face. When the tap some eejit fitted in the downstairs jacks suddenly came loose and sent a jet of water into your left eye socket, you'd sigh and resignedly get the mop and the Optrex. When the light that an electrician fitted in the living room electrocutes the cat, you'd accept it stoically and chuck the poor moggy out in the next bin collection.

Irish tradesmen are also notorious for half-doing a job and then vanishing like a fart in a hurricane. You ring them 100 times on their mobile, which always goes to voicemail, as the guy is busy half-doing a job for someone else. Actually that should probably read 'doing a job *on* someone else'. If you do manage to eventually get the scumbag, he'll give you some oul' guff about 'de plasterer I use is on holliers' or 'me wife's been in de hospital' and promise to come and fix his f**k-up the next day. Naturally he doesn't show up. And if you've been naive enough to have already paid him, your chances of ever seeing his face again are about the same as you winning the World Black Pudding Throwing Championship. (Yes, there really is such a thing.)

At this stage, you begin to devote an unhealthy amount of your time to daydreaming about the methods of torture you

Feast your eyes, ladies.

will inflict upon the guy before you finally finish the geebag off with a chainsaw.

But with the arrival of the Poles and Latvians and Lithuanians etc., the veil was suddenly lifted from our eyes. You book a guy to fix your gutter at say, 11am on a Tuesday. When he arrives at 11am on the correct Tuesday, you faint. Such a thing is unheard of in Ireland. And then he fixes the gutter. *And does it properly!* He doesn't ask for tea and bikkies, make a mess in your jacks or stop for a breather every 15 minutes. When he finishes in double-quick time (by Irish standards), so rattled are you with the shock, you have to pop a couple of Valium. He then charges you the agreed fee without any hidden extras, gives you a receipt and a phone number, and in the unlikely event you have to call him later he *actually* answers his phone!

As so much Irish tradesmen's work is often a bit of a joke, it seems appropriate to end on one:

1ˢᵗ Irish tradesman: Is the woman's u-bend leaking, Mick?

2ⁿᵈ Irish tradesman: No, Eamon, but I'm workin' on it.

24 OUR ADDICTION TO UGLY BUILDINGS

It began soon after Ireland became a republic in 1949. It was as if we'd decided that, as a complete break with our troubled past, we'd start demolishing fine buildings that were erected during the era of British dominance and replace them with modern structures that reflected our march towards the future. Unfortunately almost all of them also reflect our wojus taste in architecture. From the 1950s to the present day we continue

Breathtaking, isn't it?

to throw up lumps of concrete that aren't so much eye-*sores* as eye-*agonies*.

A measure of the nation's taste in architecture is the fact that a sizeable number of people want Dublin's two hideous Poolbeg chimney monstrosities saved from demolition as they're part of 'Dublin's heritage'. This is like saying that you don't want a pus-filled growth on your arse removed because it is a part of your very being.

But probably the building that is most regularly voted Ireland's ugliest is Dublin's Hawkins House, HQ of the Department of Health, which has a certain irony to it, considering that one glance at this deformity will leave you feeling quite ill. Its architect was one Sir Thomas Bennett, an Englishman, and you can only imagine him sniggering to himself as he persuaded the gobshites in the Department of Health to approve it in the early 1960s. He probably thought it was a way of getting the Paddies back for leaving Britain.

Then there's Liberty Hall. The original fine building was flattened by the British during the Rising. Jaysus, we could use a few of those shells now. What possessed the Dublin City Planners of the 1960s to put such a yoke, slap-bang in the centre of the capital? Hallucinogenic drugs, perhaps? The thing is, that the owner, SIPTU, planned to demolish the giant ugly stick a couple of years ago – great news – except that they intended replacing it with something just as hideous. *Ah, stop!*

Our addiction to ugliness is not limited to Dublin. A few

years after Liberty Hall was flung up, Cork decided to go one better by showing that they could outdo the Dubs with not only higher, but uglier. Up went Cork County Hall in 1968, and down went standards yet again.

Cork Opera House, a block of 1960s gank is another building that can comfortably compete with the naked mole rat as among the ugliest things on the planet. So brutal is it that they've recently put up a ginormous glass façade to hide the wojus yoke behind.

Back to Dublin and the infamous Wood Quay bunkers, now also hidden away like a deformed mad aunt behind a slightly less horrendous hodgepodge of modern architecture. It was as though the gougers in the 1970s not only decided to destroy a valuable archaeological site, but to erect a ginormous concrete block on top of it just out of badness.

These are just a few of the highlights. But our penchant for architecture so ugly it makes the zombies in 'The Walking Dead' look like supermodels is like a rash throughout the country. Sarsfield House in Limerick would have the great patriot after whom it was named denying he was Irish at all. And Waterford, Galway, Sligo and every other city, town and village in the country can boast several candidates in the manky architecture stakes.

Of course, most of these were thrown up in decades gone by. Surely we're maturing as a nation, architecturally speaking? Well, ask the residents of Dun Laoighaire what they think of

their new library. Of course, one man's eyesore is another's
Venus. Or in this case, one man's eyesore is another's Medusa.

Holy sweet Christ, will we ever learn?

25 Gaeilgeoir Gobshites

Very few Irish people have any problem with Irish speakers, and most of them actually wish they could speak Irish fluently, rather than just the *cúpla focal*. But, Jaysus, there's nothing worse than having a *Gaeilgeoir* in your face. The *Gaeilgeoir* is the guy, male or female, who'll lecture you about it being a disgrace that you can't deal with your bank '*as Gaeilge*' or that road signs should all be bilingual. (Considering that many of our road signs make no sense in English, this is like begging for disaster.)

Back when we were in school, Irish class for most of us was akin to being dragged into a torture chamber during the Spanish Inquisition. The *Gaeilgeoir* however was the guy who excelled at the language, probably because his/her Ma and Da were fluent. He/she wore a smug, superior grin as he/she

It's not pronounced telephone. It's pronounced telefón.

proudly expounded on the use of the *modh coinníollach,* until all everyone else wanted to do was tell him/her to *póg mo thoin*.

The *Gaeilgeoir* resists changes in the teaching methods of Irish, principally because they are about as useless as an ejector seat on a helicopter, which means that he/she and fellow *Gaeilgeoirí* can continue to feel superior to the rest of us poor linguistically challenged *amadáns*.

You'll be able to recognise a Gaeilgeoir from his or her name, which is usually something like Dearbhfhorghaill Ó Cuinneagáin de Prionnbhíol. He/she will also have a long, scraggly beard, a permanently serious expression and be ready to strangle you to death should you mention that you think the traditional approach to the Irish language is completely shite.

It's best to think of *Gaeilgeoirí* as the linguistic equivalent of the Taliban, except more scary. And, like those nutters, they should be avoided at all cost.

26 Pharmacy rip-offs

They'll tell you that these days are long gone. They'll tell you that Irish pharmacies are now happy to sell you generic drugs for a fraction of the price of the branded equivalent. They'll tell you that poor pharmacists are operating on wafer-thin margins and are making great sacrifices to bring the people of Ireland cheaper medicine.

What a load of oul' bollix.

Irish pharmacies are, as a rule, a bunch of rip-off gougers who should be prescribed something to induce constipation

Side effects may include drowsiness and acute shortage of cash.

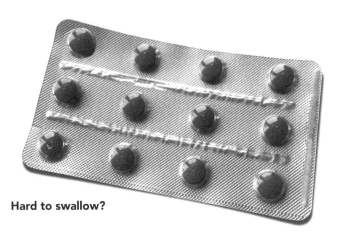

Hard to swallow?

so we don't have to endure any more of their shite. The reality is that although the scumbags are offering generic medicines, often the price they're charging is only marginally below the price for the branded equivalent. Check it out by travelling to Northern Ireland where you'll usually find these drugs for half the price! Pharmacists then give the usually guff about 'costs being higher here'. For this read 'we can get away with it here, and we're a bunch of greedy tosspots.'

But it doesn't stop at prescribed medicines. Virtually everything you'll find in an Irish pharmacy is way over-priced compared to the likes of Britain, Spain, France, Germany, or anyfeckingwhere. Nappy rash powder, underarm deodorant, mouthwash, ear wax drops, condoms, cough mixture, you name it. There is no part of your body that isn't subject to the Irish pharmacist's beady rip-off eyes.

It's enough to make you sick. Except thanks to these sleeveens, you can't afford to be.

27 Parish Pump Politicians (See also: Having the worst politicians in the western world)

One of the worst aspects of Ireland's wojus political culture is this slithery creature. These beasts – and there are almost as many of them as there are TDs in the Dáil – are like a massive stone tied around the nation's neck, dragging us back, choking us, restricting our advancement to a crawl.

It doesn't matter whether Ireland is being invaded by the Chinese Red Army or being laid waste by an alien spacecraft, the parish pump politician's principal concern is still getting planning permission for Mick O'Hara's cowshed, or moving Mrs Murphy up the hospital waiting list, so she can have her gall-bladder operation.

These cute hoors are a nationwide phenomenon. Indeed two former Taoisigh and Dubs were among the nation's biggest practitioners. They'd sit in the local pub on a weekday afternoon dispensing favours to locals like a pair of half-arsed Don Corleones, knowing that the payback comes at election time. F*** the national interest. F*** *your* mother, who got

MICHAEL O'SLIABHEEN

CONSTITUENCY CLINIC TUESDAYS 8PM

☐ PLANNING PERMISSION
☐ GRANTS
☐ WAITING LISTS
☐ CHARACTER REFS
☐ PROBLEMS SORTED
☐ BY-PASSING PROPER CHANNELS

bumped *down* the waiting list to make way for Mrs Murphy's gall bladder. F*** everyone so long as the cute hoor gets his vote and gets back into the Dáil so the whole sorry cycle can begin again.

In theory, TDs are elected to run the country. *The country*. Not the county. Not the townland. Not the parish. But in reality, TDs are elected in Ireland for their expertise in pulling strings; bypassing planning laws, fiddling the system to get someone a medical card, arranging a grant for some fecker who isn't entitled to it, having funds diverted from some urgent project to one that favours their reputation with their constituents, whether they need it or not.

So instead of looking after the greater national interest and benefitting everyone by regulating banks, introducing planning laws, abolishing public service inefficiencies, developing national infrastructural plans for the future, etc etc, our pathetic bunch of sleeveens are arranging a grant for Seamus O'Sullivan to have double glazing fitted in his downstairs jacks.

And does it matter to the voters if their local TD is an out-and-out crook? Or a corrupt scumbag who would stab you in the eye with a pencil as quick as he'd give you're the time of day? Not a bit of it. As long as good oul' Parish Pump Paddy gets me off the charge for beating the shite out of the barman when I was gee-eyed, sure he's a great fella altogether.

Really, we've only ourselves to blame.

28 THE HEALTH SERVICE

Where do you start? The HSE have provided us with enough slaggin' material to fill the Great Library of Alexandria ten times over.

But a good place to begin when considering Ireland's health service is with the wise maxim 'Don't get f**king sick in Ireland.' If you can manage this for the duration of your lifetime, then you've absolutely nothing to worry about. Alternatively, if you do get sick and have loads of dosh to splash around on overpriced health insurance, you've also got nothing to worry about (besides the fact that you might have a tumour the size of a *sliothar* in the centre of your head, that is). On the other hand, if you are not a) a cyborg or an alien being with a perfect immune system, or b) bleedin' loaded, then unfortunately you're bollixed. Sorry for the bad news.

So why, when we throw so much money at the health system is it constantly spiralling downwards? It can be summed up in two simple words: 'vested' and 'interests'. Everyone is to blame. Management, consultants, unions, doctors, nurses, lab staff, paramedics, porters, secretaries: the whole f**king lot of them. You'll hear lots of oul' guff from these vested interests about the tireless, thankless job they're doing. Pure crap. That's they job they're trained and paid for. If you don't like having to wipe some oul' lad's arse, tough shit! Why become a carer or a nurse? If you don't like wheeling some smelly oul' wan with a bad attitude down for her x-ray then why become a hospital porter?

The fact is that every section of the health service is operating at minimal efficiency levels. The systems they work to are outdated and banjaxed and nobody can be arsed changing them, probably because it might involve some inconvenience to their lives, or because it might affect the number of overtime hours they can get, or some oul' shite.

Healthcare workers will go as mad as a sack of puppies thrun' on a bonfire when they hear such observations. The government aren't putting enough money into the service, they'll scream. There are more sick people than we can deal with, they'll yell. Bollix. The proof of the pudding is in the eating, as the saying goes.

What does funding have to do with clinics starting an hour later than they're supposed to? Why do certain departments simply close down at four o'clock on a Friday afternoon? How can you have hundreds of people on trolleys when there are wards available upstairs with empty beds? Why do phone calls often go answered? Why do people turn up for consultant appointments only to be told Mr/Ms Big Shot Professor is away at a conference? Why is so much money thrown away ferrying people around in overpriced taxis? Why are contracts granted un-tendered to cronies of management? And in the name of holy sweet Mary Mother of God in heaven, why does everyone get an outpatient appointment at the same time? That fact alone is the HSE in microcosm – the perfect storm of inefficiency. It actually defies belief. It makes absolutely no sense, it inconveniences thousands of people every day, forces ill patients to sit for up to *eight hours* in brutal conditions, and results in departments and corridors being crammed with bodies, wheelchairs and germs. The only possible explanation is that the bastards running the various departments simply can't be arsed to spend time sorting out more reasonable appointment times. They're just too f**cking lazy! And these are the people who are 'working tirelessly in a thankless job' and looking for our sympathy! Some feckin' chance.

So the next time you hear some health worker bowsie, at any level, whinging about how tough their lot is, tell them then need a suppository, i.e. they can go and shove it up their arse. Oh, hang on, no, that's a bad idea. There's a two-year waiting list to have that done.

Age? Do you mean now, or when I arrived?

29 THE BRITISH CLAIMING ONE OF OURS

If there's one thing that can drive an Irish person as mad as a rabid dog in a spin dryer, it's when the British media claim for themselves someone who is obviously 110% Irish. This is usually a result of either pure ignorance or simply because they want the national kudos associated with the person's success for themselves.

The greedy feckers! It's not like our friends in Britain are short of their own success stories in sport, acting, music, art, or whatever. They've gazillions of guys who've done them proud. But here in little Ireland where we've one-fifteenth of their

population and not enough spare cash to finance an athlete's jockstrap, we tend to hold our relatively rare heroes tightly to our bosom. Katie Taylor, U2, The Corrs, Samuel Beckett, Chris O'Dowd, Colin Farrell, Barry McGuigan, Seamus Heaney and gazillions of other Paddies have all been claimed as British. Get your greedy paws off! They're all as Irish as Clonakilty Black Pudding.

Oh, and not forgetting Westlife. Although, on the other hand, every cloud has a silver lining…

30 CATHOLIC FUNDAMENTALISTS

As Gerry Adams once famously said of another bunch of loopers, 'they haven't gone away, you know.' And while the Catholic Mujahideen aren't quite as prominent as in days gone by, they're still lingering in the background, like the smell of cowshite on your shoe, and ready to oppose anything that remotely differs from their extreme right-wing view of the universe.

Younger readers may not realise how prominent these gobshites were back in the day. Their original strategy in the 1970s and '80s was, essentially, to try to stop all Irish Catholics from engaging in sex in any way, which included thinking about it. Sex was purely for the procreation of children, they screamed. When a couple of their prominent priests and bishops turned out to have taken them at their word, they became less vocal on this subject.

Catholic fundamentalists also had/have a great fear of nudity. Now, we're not necessarily talking sexual nudity here, but basically anyone being in the nip in any context causes them to have a conniption fit. Secretly, all right-wing Catholics undergo severe psychological trauma in dealing with the notion that underneath their clothes, they are all walking around naked. You see, nudity has the potential to cause one to have sinful thoughts, they believe, and therefore should be banned. But with the torrent of nudity and sex that is available on TV and the Internet these days, they have long since lost that battle.

But they had lots of other fronts they could attack. Divorce, abortion, homosexuality, contraception etc. They lost the divorce battle, despite using the equivalent of a 'dirty war', principally because they managed to piss off virtually every male in the country with their famous poster 'Hello divorce, bye bye Daddy'. Their fight to make the rhythm method the only method of contraception available was lost after thousands of couples injured themselves trying to have sex and dance to Elvis at the same time. They're holding their ground on the abortion issue, and whether you agree with it or not on religious or personal grounds, the fact is that all the right-wing nuts have really done is managed to export the matter to the UK.

Catholic Nazis can also show their sympathetic side when it comes to gay or lesbian people. They 'understand' that poor gays and lesbians are 'sick' people and need psychiatric help and drugs to make them more like 'normal people'. Ahhh, isn't that sweet of them? Of course, the odds are that a sizeable number of the Catholic Mujahideen are as gay as a flamingo with a pink feather duster. Maybe a few of them should set an example, first, by coming out, and, second, by submitting themselves to the aforementioned psychiatric/drug treatments. But let's not wait for that to happen any time soon.

And to return briefly to the contraception issue. Most people aren't aware that Catholic fundamentalists have their own built-in contraception method.

It's called their personalities.

31 Rip-off Ireland

Yes, you've already had rants about supermarkets and pharmacies and a few other examples of the great Irish rip-off game, but it's the topic that keeps on giving, so here's another one about rip-offs in general.

First off, you cannot avoid being ripped off in Ireland. It is built into our culture. It is in our genetic make-up. It may even be a part of our Constitution, although we'll have to get the lawyers to check that one out – or we could, if they weren't such a bunch of lousy rip-off merchants. But sometimes it seems that there must have been a line in the Proclamation that Padraig Pearse yelled out in 1916 that went: 'Irishmen and Irishwomen, in the name of God and of the dead generations, we declare the right of the people of Ireland to rip each other off at every conceivable opportunity, and then everyone else on the planet…'

At the time of writing, Irish prices are 18% higher than the EU average. But it's the individual examples that can really do your head in, like the coffee shop that charges enough to buy a coffee plantation for a latte and a bleedin' muffin. Or the newsagent that charges double the British price for the same

magazines. Or the directory enquiries service with the ganky jingle that charges as much for connecting you with a number around the corner as it normally costs to ring someone in Burkina Faso. Or the pubs (especially in Temple Bar, Dublin) that charge so much that you can't even get pissed.

There is no aspect of Irish life, big or small, that is untainted by these scumbags dipping their hands into our pockets. Want to heat your house? Rip-off. Need to go to your GP? Rip-off. Want to drive on a motorway? Rip-off. Rip-off. Feckin' rip-off!

If you're relying on our geebag legislators to eventually sort the problem, get ready for a long wait as they're either too cosy with many of the ripper-off-ers, too busy doing favours for locals so they'll get re-elected, or, let's be honest, they're simply too thick. We've become so used to being exploited like a bunch of gullible eejits that we think we're completely powerless. But we're not. We just need to change our attitudes.

The more we shop around the more it will piss off all the

rip-off artists. Most people, for example, renew their home/car/ health insurance automatically every year. Don't. You're being ripped off. Depend on it. Chances are that a quick on-line search will save you a packet. In fact, don't renew any contract automatically, such as your electricity or phone provider. Let them sweat until the day before renewal. You can be sure the bastards will make you a better offer. If your local coffee shop is overcharging you, stop going there for a month. If you're being overcharged for clothes (which you are), start buying some stuff online. Switch, switch, switch. You'll save enough to finance a small banana republic in South America. And more importantly, you'll cut the profits of all the rip-off slimeballs.

Actually, a good starting place is the line from the 1970s movie *Network* that goes: 'I'm as mad as hell, and I'm not going to take this anymore!' Thanks to rip-off Ireland, being as mad as hell has become part of the national psyche. Just don't stand for this shite anymore!

32 PUBLIC SERVICE WASTE

Were there an annual 'European-Throwing-Taxpayers'-Money-Down-the-Drain' Cup, we'd definitely at least reach the semis every year, and probably be the champs on a regular basis.

You see, public servants operate on a simple dictum that, when it comes to matters financial: It's not *my* money so I don't give a shite.

So let's say they need 20 new computers to replace the 20 they bought six months ago but which weren't suitable (although nobody could be arsed to check before they actually bought them). They'll contact a computer supplier who will then immediately start rubbing his hands because a call from the Irish public service is like a call from the National Lottery telling you you've hit the jackpot. The computer supplier will then charge the public servant, say, €2000 per computer and the public servant will promptly hand over a cheque. The computer supplier, now grinning like a mad yoke, will then resume selling the computers to other normal clients at their usual price of €500. The public servant may or may not know he's been ripped off – either way, he doesn't give a flyin' feck. It's not his money, after all.

Has my department bought too many periodicals that'll never see the outside of their cellophane wrapping? Who cares? Dump the lot. Someone else is paying for them. Can't find a pencil to scratch my arse with? Doesn't matter, put in an order for a box of 20. It's not my dosh. Did the taxi to my meeting around the corner cost €50? So what? It's not like someone's going to bother their hole checking.

This public service palaver goes from the bottom right to the top. That new Pathology Office we were building? The one where we made a bollix of the planning and the building contractor procurement, and now we've had to demolish it? Never mind, it's only a little over €3 mill, and its not like anyone's going to be demoted or fired, is it?

Ah yes, guys, just keep on spending taxpayer's money like there's no tomorrow!

But guess what? It's tomorrow.

89

33 GETTING THE THIRD DEGREE WHEN YOU BUY SOLPADEINE

You've got a massive hangover after a night on the tear and on the way to work you wander into a pharmacy. There's a girl of 19 standing behind the counter with a ring in her nose and a tattoo of a skull on her neck, i.e. she does not appear on first glance to be a qualified medical professional.

'Pack of Solpadeine, please.'

Her smile disappears and she suddenly takes on the demeanour of an SS Obergruppenführer. It's like you've just asked her for crack cocaine.

'What do you want it for?' she snaps.

There are other customers waiting. You head throbs. You feel under pressure. You don't want to admit to a child that you were so rat-arsed last night that you feel like a jockey's jockstrap.

'Eh…eh…'

'What do you need the Solpadeine for?' she barks like you're a three-year-old who's asked for matches and a can of petrol.

What you really want to say is 'F*** off, you silly bitch and mind your own f***ing business!' Instead you mutter 'Em, I've a sore …eh…back.'

'There are other drugs I can give you for that.'

'But I don't want…'

'Are you a druggie?'

'What? No, I've just got a bleedin' hangover, you stupid wagon!'

Of course the last bit is fictional, yet really that's what is implied by these public interrogations.

But it's not the poor girl's/guy's fault. It's all down to the Pharmaceutical Society of Ireland. Yes, they're the gobshites responsible for this ill-thought out oul' bollix. In theory, it is to reduce addiction to codeine among the masses. All very noble. So what is supposed to happen, according to their own rules, is that when you ask for a brand containing codeine the pharmacist is supposed to be summoned, who will then take you to a private consultation area and discuss the matter with

It's for my unmentionable
female problems.

CHEMIST

you. Still a pain in the backside, but at least you don't have to be humiliated in public. In practice, of course, pharmacists can't bother their arse doing this, so they just leave it to the shop attendant to ask you for private medical information in front of half the shop.

And, of course, it has zero effect on codeine addicts as they'll simply lie about what they need the drug for and the poor sap behind the counter will have no choice but to believe him/her. Net result? No effect on codeine addicts and members of the public genuinely in need of painkillers are humiliated and left to suffer. Yeah, the stupid feckers really thought that one through.

Actually, what happened here was that someone higher up the chain said 'boo' to the PSI about codeine being sold over the counter. But instead of actually sorting out the problem, the PSI just passed the responsibility buck to the pharmacies.

So the next time you're grilled by some shop assistant about your private medical condition, be it period pains, back pain, a sports injury or whatever, be ready with something like this:

'I've recently had surgery on my penis/vagina which has resulted in a great deal of swelling and throbbing pain, and that's made it hard for me to engage in sexual intercourse, and besides that, I've also got a large growth on my a...'

By this point, the poor, scarlet-faced assistant will be shoving the Solpadeine or Nurofen Plus in your face for free, and ushering you out the door.

34 WHY DO YOU HARDLY EVER SEE THE GARDAÍ PATROLLING THE STREETS?

Take a trip to New York, London, Paris, Amsterdam, Copenhagen or any modern city nowadays and you'll find the local cops wandering the streets, especially around the touristy areas. So naturally, in Ireland, Gardaí on the streets are about as scarce as virgins in a swingers club.

International studies have been carried out that show the benefits of having a visible police presence on the streets include a deterrent to unsociable and criminal behaviour, increased sense of security among the public, improved relationships between police and community, and even considerable savings to Joe Public on petrol and vehicle maintenance. So the old-fashioned Garda-on-the-beat makes perfect common sense. But, of course, most of Ireland's policymakers operate on the principle of doing the diametric opposite of what common sense demands. Making a hames of everything is the Irish way!

O'Connell Street, Dublin, is symptomatic of the same problems you'll find in Tralee, Cork, Sligo or anywhere in the country. For decades people have been calling for more Gardaí on the capital's main street, especially after dark. You'll find enough quotes from government ministers promising 'tough, decisive action' to fill an industrial skip. Yet, the Gardaí never arrive. Citizens and tourists regularly have the shite kicked out of them by drunken or drug-addled yahoos wandering around in gangs as if they own the place. O'Connell Street, like many city or town centre, has practically become a no-go area after dark, unless you're accompanied by a troop of Mossad-trained personal bodyguards carrying Uzi sub-machine guns.

What is it that ministers and senior Gardaí don't get? Are we as a nation missing something that only those in command know about? Are we too dim to understand some brilliant longer-term policy? You must be joking. More likely that they haven't a feckin' clue how to run a police force effectively. They'll whinge that they haven't the resources, of course. Thing is, they had the resources back in the great Celtic Tiger days – and there still weren't any Gardaí on the bleedin' streets.

In Ireland, a citizen's lot is not a happy one.

35 COUNCILS ISSUING WATER-LEVEL WARNINGS IN ONE OF THE WETTEST PLACES ON EARTH

Yes, it's all tied up with the water tax fiasco and the government will tell you that the reason we need your spondulics is to fix the creaking water infrastructure. All very well, but really, seriously, we've been hearing this oul' guff for decades and we have to ask, how in the name of the holy sainted mother can Ireland, the wettest place in Europe, be perennially short of water?

It's a burst pipe outside number 62 ...

An Irish reservoir

Here in Ireland, brutal as the weather can be, it does provide us with about 1300mm of water every year. But you can be sure that after three days without a cloudburst, your local county council will be issuing dire warnings about us all dying horribly of thirst if we don't conserve water.

Now, take Perth in Western Australia, the driest city in one of the driest continents on Earth. They have an annual rainfall of about 600mm, less than half ours. A scorching sun beats down for nine months of the year and you could fry a sausage on the roof of your bleedin' car on most days. Yet the parks are bursting with life and boast grass to rival an Irish field in November. Sprinklers explode into action every day onto the plants and the people. Fountains sparkle in the sunlight, jets of water dance in the breeze. Children splash in outdoor pools and icy water pours from the city's taps in a never-ending flow. But how is this all possible? How can we have more than twice the rain of Perth and still sometimes not have enough water to wash the wax out of our ears?

Unfair comparison, you may say. Perth is bleedin' rolling in dosh. Perhaps, but let's try somewhere with an equally ganky mess of an economy. Spain, for example. Annual rainfall: less than 600mm per annum. Most of us have been there. You've seen the water shooting from the taps at the height of summer, you've seen the fountains, the pools, the guys washing the street with power hoses in the morning. How can they do it? Have they some magic formula for manufacturing water out of thin air?

Morocco. Average rainfall, 350mm. Granted, not everyone is connected to the water supply, but most people are, and farmers have to use massive amounts of water to irrigate their fields – not a problem we have. Morocco loses 30% of their piped water through leaks – and we lose 50%! Germany loses 5%, Denmark 10%, the UK and Spain 20%. Feckin' Romania only loses 28%!

So, to those in charge of our little nation, here's a secret. Gather around and listen carefully, dear ministers and planners, because you can apply this magic to a whole range of things and save the country billions in the future. It's an old concept but you obviously aren't familiar with it. It's called 'planning ahead'. Do you need that repeated or explained in any way?

Ah, forget it. Better start stockpiling water now for the three-day drought in July, and the July after that, and the one after that….

36 THE ROSE OF TRALEE LOVELY GIRLS FESTIVAL

The Rose of Tralee annual festival is not a beauty pageant with a swimwear section for dirty oul' lads. No, it's all about the girls' personalities – or so the organisers claim.

Let's be honest here. It's not about the girls' personalities. It's about earning loads of dosh on the back of projecting a sexist, old-fashioned image of Irish women as sweet, virginal cailíns.

'It is not a beauty contest, it is an INNER beauty contest,' screams the RoT website. So, in theory, if you've got a pointy nose, big ears, crossed eyes, spots, bald patches and a moustache, you're still in with a shout to become the next Rose of Tralee! Well, so long as you're really, *really* nice underneath your ganky exterior.

If it's an 'inner beauty' contest, why no size 14+ women? We have to assume that the organisers believe only girls with thin-yet-curvy bottoms have personalities. Oh, and you have to be younger than 28 because, after that, you've obviously got no personality at all. You also have to be single. That's ostensibly because the girl in the song was single, although the lyrics don't specifically state this, and for all we know the lovely and fair cailín of the tune was just having a bit on the side. You know those Kerry wans. The 'single rule' also lets us glimpse one of the other reasons behind the parade of girls – to line them up as a prospective match with some head-the-ball. A little bit like choosing a cow at public auction, in fact. Exactly how the modern Irish woman wants to be depicted to the watching world!

But be warned if you choose to watch the competition next time it's on – there is a rumour, probably true, that thousands of the men and women who watched it last time have had to undergo facial reconstruction to have their cringes removed. You have been warned.

I'm sorry, but the judges felt you didn't have enough inner beauty.

37 RETURNING EMIGRANTS BACK ON HOLIDAYS MOANING ABOUT IRELAND

The following conversation will sound familiar to an awful lot of people:

Colm: Great to see you again, Peter. How's Australia/London/New York/Germany etc?

Peter: Brilliant. Would you not think about moving over yourself?

Colm: Nah. Like it here.

Peter: *Really?* (Spoken like Colm's just said he'd like to be burned alive.)

Colm: Yeah.

Peter: But everything's so crap here. The taxes are so high. And everything's twice the price it is in Australia/London/New York/Germany etc. The restaurants here are shite and the girls are all ugly wagons compared to the babes in Australia/London/New York/Germany etc. You should think about it.

Colm: Yeah, maybe.

Peter: But really. I mean, look at the roads here for example. They're like dirt tracks compared to the ones in Australia/London/New York/Germany etc. And then there's the pay.

Jaysus you can earn a fortune in Australia/London/New York/ Germany etc. And the weather? I mean I didn't realise I had a tan until I came home and saw all the pasty-faced gobshites here. Aw, look, it's raining again. Now you'd never get *that* in summer in Australia/London/New York/Germany etc.

Colm: (Trying to think of an excuse to leave.) Listen, I've got an appointment…

Peter: That reminds me. I must make an appointment with a chiropodist. My feet are killing me. Oh, wait, do you have chiropodists in Ireland?

Colm: Eh, yeah…

Peter: Anyway, I was saying. Do you not get bored out

We will shortly be landing at Dublin Airport. Would passengers refrain from giving out shite about Ireland until the plane arrives at the terminal.

of your head here? 'Cause in Australia/London/New York/ Germany etc, there's so much to do, besides just getting pissed.

Colm: That right?

Peter: Still, we must meet for a pint, seeing as that's all everyone does for craic here.

Colm: Meet you for a pint? I'd rather have hot needles inserted into my eyeballs...

Yes, all too familiar. Did you know how you can tell when a plane full of visiting emigrants has just landed in Ireland? Yep, when the engine stops, you can still hear the whine of the passengers.

38 ELECTION POSTER MANIA

Every couple of years, when there's an election for something or other, the country gets swamped under a gazillion posters of grinning gobshites eager to win your favour. There is no other country in Europe that indulges in the orgy of postering that us poor Micks have to endure. Every lamp post from Kerry to Dublin to Donegal is obliterated by a collection of grinning, hairy brutes – and that's just the women candidates. Breathtaking scenery is scarred by the politicians' ugly mugs and baloney slogans, while streetscapes vanish under the forest of paper and plastic.

But believe it or not, things used to be far worse. Many can remember the day when the bastards used to slap up posters anywhere they fancied using *wallpaper paste*. You'd end up having to look at the greasy gobdaw for literally years.

They've changed to the tie-up method, using those plastic-tie yokes to attach them to poles. But being Irish politicians, they didn't act with any sense of responsibility, and never bothered their arse taking the bleedin' things down. It took a change in the law to force their hand – and that in itself tells us a lot about our political candidates. Now the sleeveens can only

put up posters 30 days before an election and must remove them within seven days afterwards. But many cute hoors have come up with a way around the regulations. If your poster also advertises a meeting of some sort, such as a 'Politician'll-Fix-It'-type clinic, they're not deemed to be election posters. Then they simply whip off the clinic bit and bob's your uncle, election poster. If you see any of the jammy hoors doing this next time, resolve not to vote for them.

The other problem is with the plastic ties. The rules say the posters have to be removed, but not the plastic yokes. So, when the time comes, the lazy yahoos simply rip the poster off the pole and leave the plastic ties there. Result – every pole in Ireland now sports about fifty ugly white plastic ties.

By the way, has there ever been any research to show that these posters have ever had even the teensiest weensiest effect on who anyone votes for? No, of course not. So, in other words, it's all just a big waste of paper, time and money.

But if the eejits feel they have to advertise in this way, can't we limit the number of posters every candidate is allowed? Honestly, they're a feckin' blight on the whole country.

And the posters are a feckin' blight as well.

39 IRISH PEOPLE MISUSING THE WORD 'LITERALLY'

Ok, this is not just limited to Irish people, but we're literally at the top of the tree, competing to make 'literally' the most misused word in the English language.

Politicians on the radio are particular misusers:

'I'll tell you Pat, if there's no Dáil debate on the matter, I'll literally explode.' We'd better hope there's a Dáil debate then, or the whole kip'll be covered in the cute hoor's guts.

Our sports presenters and commentators are literally as bad as that. Take this, for example:

'Oh, the Kilkenny full-back literally handed it to Tipp on a golden platter.' So, eh, let's get this straight then… the Kilkenny full-back suddenly whipped out a golden tray from somewhere, placed the *sliothar* on it and presented it to his opponent?

Here's another sporting example:

'Messi literally tore the defenders to pieces!' Wow! Was he arrested for mass murder? Were there players limbs littering the Nou Camp?

Our TV chat show hosts are also expert at misusing the

word: 'So tell me, Jean, when he left you, were you literally crushed to a pulp?' Of course she wasn't, you moron! She's not a big yucky blob on the chair opposite you!

But few remain untarnished. Here are a few more examples:

Journalists: 'The energy regulator has literally sold each of us a pig in a poke.' Really? When are all our pigs being delivered?

Musicians: 'This album is literally going to blow the whole world away.' Better say our prayers quick then.

Literary critics: 'The prose in Gibson's novel literally twists the heart into a knot.' Steer clear of that book, then, or your f***ed.

News commentators: 'When the jury's decision was read out, the packed courtroom literally went insane.' Wow! The nuthouse will be jammers.

And so on and so forth. The nation is drowning in misused 'literallys'. For the sake of the spoken and written word, will all of these gobshites please stop talking through their arses? Figuratively speaking, of course.

He had a neck quite literally like a jockey's backside.

40 Why have the bankers gotten off scot-free after the economic collapse?

There are many who argue that none of the actions that brought about the banking collapse, which cost enough money for us to have started our own space program, was actually illegal. This is the reason why no one has been sent to prison for one of the greatest economic collapses in the history of the world.

Then there are others who say that's a big pile of steaming shite, although they may express it differently.

The main argument put forward by those who say the bastards shouldn't be in prison is that the bankers were merely guilty of stupidity and greed, which are not illegal, otherwise most of our elected representatives would be in the slammer. Nobody would argue with the latter, as they were undoubtedly the greediest shower of savages on the planet, but stupid they were not. Does anyone believe for a moment that these shitehawks didn't know precisely what they were up to and what was going on in the world? Somehow it seems that in

For the same money...

Ireland, trading recklessly is ok. Not to mention the whole rake of other murky goings-on that we'll never hear about.

But with the State imposing the toughest austerity measures in our history on the populace, surely it would be in the Government's interest to show they were determined to crack down on white-collar scumbags? You'd imagine they'd be all gung-ho to show us all that justice would be served, so the public could at least have the satisfaction of metaphorically yelling abuse at the gougers on their way to the guillotine. Yes, in any normal country that would be the case.

Yet in 2012, three years after the collapse, a High Court judge said he found it 'extraordinary' that only eleven Gardaí had been assigned to investigate the dodgy shenanigans at Anglo Irish Bank. You and us both, Your Honour.

The fact is that, to this day, after all

that's happened, our system for dealing with financial crooks is as useless as an ashtray on a motorbike. One startling statistic that underlines this is that of almost 700 potential financial crimes reported to the Gardaí over a four-year period, just two prosecutions resulted. TWO!

You have to wonder why there is so little appetite in the circles of power to change this situation. And then again, maybe you don't really have to wonder about it too much. Simply apply a little common sense.

Seriously, would you bite the hand that feeds you?

41 THE GREAT IRISH DENTIST SCAM

It's no secret that the field of study that requires the most Leaving Cert points is dentistry. Not medicine or agriculture or technology or any of a hundred other qualifications that would contribute a great deal more to society than a row of shining pearly whites. The reason for this is nothing to do with a deeply held childhood calling to go out and save the nation's chompers, but because, for generations in Ireland, it has been the fastest track to making loads and loads of dosh. We are long past the point where anyone actually studies to be a dentist because the subject interests them. No, dentists become dentists in Ireland because your little cert on the wall grants them a licence to financially kick us poor eejits in the teeth. When you compare prices with the UK, it's enough to set your teeth on edge.

A crown or a filling in the south costs about half of what it does in Northern Ireland. Half! We're talking hundreds of euros here. If you travel to eastern Europe the cost can be as little as a third of Irish prices.

Why are Irish dentists so feckin' dear? Ah, God, the usual tedious oul' shite is spewed out about higher costs here and less government support and so on and so on, *ad infinitum*, until you're fed up to your back teeth and just want to punch the nearest dentist's kisser.

If you think about what any company or practising professional's major costs are, the answer is staff wages, and the argument is often made that wages are higher here. This itself is a load of crap since the recession. But even if you accept this as an excuse, what staff costs does a dentist have? A dental nurse? That's one. Perhaps a shared receptionist, if it is a big practice? So that's a fraction of a wage. And you can be sure the cute hoors aren't paying these unfortunates top dollar – more like minimum wage. So, in effect, their main overheads come to the equivalent of a few root canals, an implant or two and a bunch of fillings! So, dentists, stop lying through your feckin' teeth!

Why can't they just spit it out and admit that the real reason

I'm giving you double the anaesthetic to ease the pain of the amount I'm going to rip you off.

it's so dear here is because they can get away with it. Nothing more. It's a big scam. A swindle. A rip-off. All designed to line their pockets with spondulicks. Remember this the next time you're sitting in that chair looking up at the with your gob open – the man hovering over you is a total gouger whose only interest is extracting as much money as he can from your pocket. At least that thought should be enough to distract you from the pain.

42 KIDS RUNNING AROUND THE PUB WHILE THEIR PARENTS GET RAT-ARSED

There is a certain type of gobshite in Ireland who is delighted to take full advantage of our very liberal laws regarding the presence of children in pubs. At present, it is legal to take kids under 15 into the pub between 10.30 in the morning and 9.00 at night. And there are a sizeable number of shitehawks who are happy to make the maximum use of the ten and a half hours' drinking time, or a sizeable chunk of it.

The result, especially at weekends, is that while the Ma and Da and their friends slowly get gee-eyed, the kids are left to their own devices for hours and eventually revert to the feral state of our prehistoric ancestors. This usually involves the little darlings crawling under other people's tables, throwing beer mats, having crisp fights, climbing on chairs, emptying salt cellars into unsuspecting drinkers' pints, peeing on people's cars in the car park, climbing on car bonnets, screaming at the top of their lungs and running around like their arses are on fire.

Brief calm is restored while they eat some chicken nuggets and chips, after which the parents resume sculling their pints and the little treasures resume their hyperactivity, now armed with sachets of tomato ketchup, mayonnaise and vinegar, which they burst and shoot at each other and everyone else.

Come 9pm, they have to vacate the place, thanks be to Christ, but by then they are in such a wojus state that they have to be carried home screaming, and thrown into bed. And that's just the parents.

43 THE SHAMELESS LACK OF ACCOUNTABILITY

The basis of our political system in Ireland is non-accountability. Not officially of course. But everyone in politics, State employment, white-collar private business and various other groups know that, basically, they can get away with all sorts of seriously dodgy dealings and nobody's going to say boo to them. Or at the very worst, someone saying boo to them is the full extent of the reprimand they're going to get.

The banking collapse is the most obvious example of Ireland's aversion to accountability. Instead of identifying those behind

The buck does not stop here.

it and giving the citizens of Ireland some sense of justice, the powers that be merely shook their heads sadly and sent the bankers off to play a game of golf.

But the scene had long been set for the bankers to get a 'Do not go to jail' card – because the greatest practitioners of evading accountability are the sleeveens in government themselves. Power in Leinster House has become incredibly centralised and hierarchal, thanks to the whip system, which forces every TD to toe the line or else they'll find their arses kicked out of the party.

This means that the gougers in cabinet can essentially do anything they want, whether it benefits the country, or merely benefits themselves or one of their buddies, and nobody can do a feckin' thing about it. And if someone decides to ask them *why*, say, a particular constituency has been favoured with a new swimming pool, or a particular crony has been appointed to a board, they just reply with a pile of oul' bull that doesn't in any way explain their behaviour – and that's the end of that.

This has always been the way in Ireland and, naturally, there has been a trickle-down effect. If there's no accountability in government, why should civil or public servants be any different?

It doesn't matter how you screw up, whether it's wasting a couple of mill on some idiotic project or fiddling your phone expenses for ten years, you know nobody's ever going to kick your arse, and you're certainly never going to lose your job.

The non-accountability bug has long since spread to those not *in*, but *closest to* government – the guys with all the money. If you're a person on minimum wage who forgets to pay his/her TV licence, you've a much greater chance of ending up in jail than a geebag in a nice suit who hides millions in an offshore account to evade tax.

The only nod to accountability in Ireland is the Public Accounts Committee, which can summon various wasters, cute hoors, gougers and gobdaws to answer for their behaviour. The problem is that even if they're shown to be as bent as a €7 note, the worst that's going to happen to them is that they'll be a bit embarrassed in public. And, since most of these yahoos have a neck like a jockey's bollocks, a bit of embarrassment isn't going to turn them off their Dom Perignon.

Until the day that Ireland has real accountability with real consequences – i.e. you get the boot with no cushy settlement, you lose your pension, you go to jail, you lose your seat in the Dáil – then the bastards are going to keep screwing the country, and let the rest of us suffer the consequences. Don't hold your breath.

44 TWINNING TOWNS

You've probably noticed the plethora of road signs around the country that proclaim that the town or village you're entering is twinned with some other town or village, usually somewhere in Europe or the Americas. But have you ever asked yourself why?

The notion of 'twinning' started after WWII and, in theory, it was a noble idea – the British, Germans, French, Americans, Italians and so on could kiss and make up again after they'd been batin' the shite out of each other for six years. But why is the practice so rampant in Ireland, which was neutral during the war?

The official reason is that twinning promotes goodwill among nations, fosters cultural exchange and encourages tourism. All very honourable, selfless and virtuous of the councillors to arrange. So can we assume that, since Carrick-on-Shannon was twinned with the village of Cesson Sévigné in Brittany over a decade ago, hordes of French people have been spending loads of dosh and teaching all the locals to speak French and cook *poulet* à *la Bretonne* and *crêpes suzette*? Or that hordes of Italians have been pouring into Cobh from Potenza Picena in sunny Italia, throwing money around and teaching the locals how to sing Puccini's *La Bohème*? Yeah? Well, there's about as much chance of that happening as you have of being decapitated by a soggy beermat.

The real reason for twinning, as we all know, is so a bunch of Irish councillors, along with their equally craic-loving counterparts abroad, can spend loads of taxpayers' money on junkets, usually to sunny or exotic places. They will argue that the EU provides grants for this sort of nonsense so the Irish taxpayer isn't bearing the full cost of boozy weekends in five-star hotels. Well, that's ok then, so long as they're wasting someone else's cash. Not.

It is a rare thing, you may not be surprised to learn, to come across an Irish town twinned with some really wojus, cold and miserable kip in Ukraine or northern Scandinavia. Instead, we prefer our piss-ups, sorry, cultural exchanges to be with towns where the climate is balmy, our favoured destinations being the US, or pretty little hamlets in France and Italy.

And many a town and city has been blessed with

multiple twinnings, such is the councillors' craving for peace and harmony among nations. Among the leaders are Limerick with eight 'twins', Killarney with seven, Clonmel, Dublin and Cork with six each, and Castlebar and Naas, with five. But the All Ireland champion by a long stretch is Galway, which seems to be on a 'world twinning tour'. The good taxpayers of that fine city are best friends with no fewer than *eleven* other towns spread over four continents. And, you know, it's often hard to get a hotel room in Galway for all the tourists from Qingdao in Shandong in Eastern China.

Money well spent, lads!

The Scots show us how it's done.

45 WOJUS DRIVERS

It is probably true that Irish people's innate ability to drive a car is no worse or better than that of most nationalities. Where we differ is that in Ireland, traditionally, crap drivers have been allowed to get away with all kinds of shite, and so our forefathers' lousy habits have been passed on from generation to generation. So, like our freedom to vote and to have basic healthcare, we regard it as a sacred right to drive like psychos, simpletons or arrogant geebags.

Where we excel in our incompetence is on the motorway. These great national thoroughfares have only really been around a couple of decades in Ireland, so we haven't quite gotten the hang of them yet. It is quite common to see complete morons stopping in the hard shoulder and then opening their door out into the left lane and clambering out to have a stretch. Every now and again the sap is stretched alright – along 100m of tarmac, having being splattered by a passing juggernaut.

Then there's the popular Irish game of motorway hopscotch. This involves two eejits overtaking each other repeatedly to show what cool dudes they are. It's a bit like cock-fighting but without the benefit of the cock's walnut-sized brain.

There is also one concept that the Celtic brain seems incapable of grasping – *the overtaking lane*. It seems simple enough on paper. The lane on the left is for driving and the lane on the right is for overtaking only. Yes, this will come as a shock to most Irish people. Overtaking only. Not for driving. Not for listening to Ian Dempsey or Newstalk Sport. Not for looking at the scenery. Not for preventing other drivers from overtaking. Not for having a fag while you sing along badly to *Stairway to Heaven*. It's for overtaking! Pull out. Overtake. Pull back in. That's all there is to it. The key phrase being 'Pull back in'. Arrrrgggghhh!

And, while we're on the subject, overtaking via the hard shoulder is another favourite in Ireland. These overtakers often

end up in the hands of undertakers.

Then there's the safe driving distance. Internationally, the three-second rule is used to gauge a safe distance, that is, it should take you a minimum of three seconds to traverse the distance to the car in front of you. In Ireland, this is known as the tenth-of-a-second rule, as a great number of gobshites, whether on motorways or elsewhere, seem to believe they can safely stop, even if they are so close to your car they can see a bleedin' pimple on the back of your neck.

These are just a handful of the highlights. So remember this the next time you take to the highways – it takes nearly 10,000 bolts to assemble a car, but just one feckin' nut to spread it all over the road.

46 The Way There's No Such Thing As Just Having Your Car Serviced

In order to prolong the life of your car and get the optimum performance from it, experts tell us to have the car serviced at least yearly. But for Irish people, taking the car to the garage is avoided in the same way as a visit to the dentist for a root canal, or a stay in hospital for a colonoscopy. The pain is of a different sort, of course, involving, as it does, the extraction of very large amounts of dosh from your bank account.

Most Irish garages display big ugly signs that scream 'Service from just €90!' Great. That sounds reasonable, you think. So you drop the car in, pop back a few hours later whistling happily to yourself, only to be greeted by Seamus, the grim-faced mechanic.

'When I was doing the service, I noticed a few problems. 'Fraid your right front sprocket angliser torsion belt has deviated from the traction slippage wheel,' he says, shaking his head as he looks mournfully down at your car.

'Ye wha?' you reply, wondering what f***ing language he's speaking.

'Ye could leave it like that, but any day it could go and

'fpssst…'

He draws his finger across his throat to indicate your imminent death.

'How much is it to fix?' you stammer.

'Let's see. About €220.'

'Ahhh for f…'

'I also saw a bit of a problem with the upper camble-spigot cable where it joins the injection suspension muffler.'

'You did?'

'And then you really need to have that distributor crank plunger solenoid fitted with a barometric tappet manifold or you could be in trouble.'

'But I only bought the car las…'

'That's the problem with these German/French/Japanese cars. See, their timing shaft combustion bracket corbangles can't cope with Irish conditions so the cylinder intake gasket springs tend to come loose from the compressor flywheel grognut … eh…winkles. Know what I mean?'

'Eh…yeah.…how much for…?

'It'll come to €1522. And 60 cent.'

'Holy Jaysus!'

'But seeing as you're a regular customer, we'll round it down to €1522 even. Can't say fairer than that, eh?'

47 THE 'GOLDEN HANDSHAKE' CULTURE

In Ancient Rome, the punishment for a commander who failed in his duty, but who otherwise behaved honourably, was usually exile. If he was dishonourable, he could expect to be stripped of his citizenship and all his possessions, and might even get a flogging or be branded with hot irons.

In modern Ireland, we've obviously evolved beyond such barbarity, and were Irish standards to be applied to Ancient Rome, the commander who'd just returned from having his arse kicked in Gaul and losing 50,000 men and half of the Empire's annual tax income, would then be given a large estate near

As your performance as CEO has been so dire, we're giving you a Platinum Handshake.

Antium, complete with a luxurious seaside villa, a few million sesterces and a bunch of slave girls to help him pass the time. In other words, if you had applied Ireland's methods to Ancient Rome, the Roman Empire would have collapsed in a week.

See, the way the system works here, so long as you're high up in political, property or financial circles, is that if you are proven to be a useless git who's as thick as a horse's mickey or as crooked as a bent corkscrew, you're made! And the bigger your failure the more spondulicks you're going to be handed. This especially applies if you're involved in banking, as all you have to do is be so wojusly brutal at your job that you bankrupt, not only the bank, but also the entire economy. If you can manage that you're almost certain to be given a nice little departure gift, like, say, €3m. Yes, folks, that's a fact.

Almost as good a gig is to become the guy responsible for regulating the banks because, after you've royally banjaxed *them* through incompetence and cronyism and become one of the key movers in the destruction of the Irish economy, the government will pay you €630,000 and a nice fat annual pension of €142,000. Otherwise, as the government kindly explained to the rest of us, you might take them to court!

Then let the f`***`er take us to court, we reply!

Being the head of a public service body who's involved in dodgy dealings and massive waste of public resources is a great way to make money in Ireland. Sure the government will happily give you hundreds of thousands plus a huge pension.

All you have to do is say the magic words 'legal action' and government will put their tails between their legs and hand over the jackpot.

Incompetence as Taoiseach or as a cabinet minister also brings great rewards. Brian Cowen, who led the abortive attack on Gaul, sorry, who played a leading role in maintaining the culture of cute hoorism that led to the culture of outright corruption that led to the culture of unfettered greed that led to the banking collapse, was allowed to ride off into the sunset with more than €300,000 of your money. The rest of his cabinet cronies were also handsomely rewarded for selling their country out to a bunch of shyster financiers and property speculators just so they could cling to power.

All of this is in the past, though. Like Ancient Rome, it's ancient history. The days of the golden handshake for sleeveens is long gone. Or so the government tells us.

Then how in the name of sweet holy God did the guy at the head of the CRC, which was rifling public donations to pay his buddies huge top-ups and lavish expenses, end up getting a pay-off of more than €700,000?

The real reason? In Ireland it's not so much the golden handshake that's the problem, as the *golden circle*.

Maybe the Ancient Romans had the right idea after all.

48 'WHAT WILL YOU BE READING THIS SUMMER?' NEWSPAPER AND RADIO FEATURES

Every year around May or June, most Irish national newspapers and radio stations run these features where they ask a bunch of 'celebrities' what books they'll be reading on the beach on their holliers. These celebrities come from all walks of life; politicians, writers, actors, sportspeople, television show hosts, journalists and so on. And they all have one thing in common – they're all a big bunch of lying shites.

'So Minister, what book will you be reading this summer?'

'I've always admired *Lord Jim* by Conrad. That and a book about market economics in the Victorian era.'

What a pile of codology. He'll be re-reading a John Grisham, like he always does.

'And you, Deirdre, what does a well-known actress, such as yourself, take to read on the beach?'

'A book about the future of feminism in the internet age.'

Like feck she will – she'll be reading *Handcuffs and Silk* or *Spank Me Please, Sir!* or similar.

'Megan, what does a TV personality like yourself enjoy by the pool?'

'This year, I'm really looking forward to getting stuck into *A History of the Qing Dynasty.*'

Absolute arseology. She'll have her nose in *The Da Vinci Code.*

'And Brian, I suppose you'll be enjoying a good sports book?'

'No actually, I'm planning to read *Moby Dick* by Melville.'

Yeah? For *Moby Dick* read *Blood Lust of the Vampire Hunters.* And he won't even finish that.

As any Irish person who's bumped into one of these poor saps while on holiday can tell you, almost without exception, they are deep into some entertaining piece of brain-candy, just like everyone else – and that, if discovered, they scramble to conceal their real reading matter inside their swimming togs.

So the next time you see one of these lists in the paper, or hear one of these discussions on the radio, treat it like what it really is: pure pulp fiction.

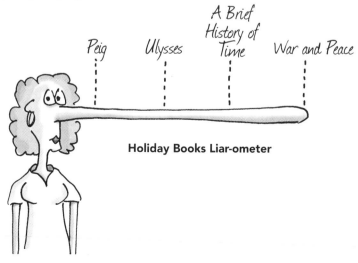

Holiday Books Liar-ometer

49 MACHINES TALKING TO US IN FOREIGN ACCENTS

You scan a tin of beans and place it on the metal shelf in the self-service area of the supermarket. Unfortunately the thing didn't scan properly and next thing a woman with a posh British accent announces: 'Unexpected item in the bagging area.'

You finish your shopping, leave the supermarket and climb into the lift to return to the car park. The lift speaks to you in an American drawl: 'Please stand clear of the doors.'

Down in the car park you stick your ticket into the paypoint yoke. Another disembodied voice, this time with a Birmingham accent, tells you: 'Please insert payment.'

You plug in your sat nav to direct you to the nearest petrol station. A woman who seems to be from Hartlepool tells you to: 'Turn right onto Grey-gew-nam-an-ag (Graiguenamanagh) Road.'

You get home and have to ring your mobile phone company. A machine that was apparently raised in New York answers: 'Please select from the following menu. For accounts, press one....'

Can it really be that hard to put an Irish person's voice into these talking contraptions, before we all start sounding like Yanks and Brits? And apparently the next generation of home appliances are going to be talking to us as well. Yes, soon your fridge will be saying: 'Oi, mate, you're runnin' low on chow, me ol' mucker.' Your washing machine will greet you thus: 'Howdy pardner, so y'all fixin' te do some laundry now?' Not to mention your oven, which will announce: 'G'day sport! I'm your Billabong 2000, the oven that beats the bardy blues!'

Someone, please pull the plug before it's too late!

50 Making lawyers rich on useless tribunals

In the last couple of decades, Ireland has spent roughly €500m on tribunals of inquiry investigating various corrupt cute hoors. This suggests we either have a great deal of corruption or that the government is being ripped-off like a bunch of naïve gobdaws.

Sadly, both of these are true. The culture of Irish politics and business that encourages cute hoorism, cronyism, brown envelopeism and screw-the-citizenism means that the well of corruption will never run dry. And, meanwhile, the tribunal gravy train has been making millionaires of sleeveen Irish lawyers quicker than the national lottery.

Arriving at a tribunal near you

Sorry, luv, I don't do tribunals.

The ironic thing is that the tradition of wasting vast sums of money on tribunals, which ostensibly set out to uncover corruption and incompetence, actually encourages it instead. See, in other sane countries where commonsense operates, they use things called laws, courts, judges, sentences and prison to handle these matters. In Ireland, various governments have deemed that certain types of citizen should not be subjected to the indignity of such a process, i.e. former political or business cronies of their own. And as tribunals have no power to send anyone to prison or even to fine them tuppence ha'penny, essentially all their gouger buddies know they have nothing to fear.

Think of the Irish tribunal system like this: all the corrupt feckers are on one football team, and all us honest citizens are on the other. The government announce with great fanfare that they're buying Lionel Messi to play on the citizens' team. Absolutely deadly, you think! But then they play Messi in goal. So the feckers beat us five-nil, and the lawyers take home all the bleedin' gate receipts.

51 Cyclists Being a Law Unto Themselves

The first thing Irish cyclists will do when there's any complaint about their behaviour is to go on a rant about how crap Irish motorists are. But as there's already a piece about our brutal driving in this book, tough shit, it's your turn, Mr or Ms Cyclist.

Irish cyclists are almost immune to all forms of legislation. That fact is based on the number of cycling offences committed annually versus the number of prosecutions, which is roughly in the ratio of 56 trillion to one. This perceived legal immunity gives cyclists the sense that that are also immune to the impact of trucks, cars and pedestrians.

For non-cyclists or anyone thinking of taking it up, here's a brief guide to Irish cyclists' understanding of various cycling/motoring terminology.

Red light: A district where hookers ply their trade.

Lamps: Things with shades that sit on your coffee table.

Reflector: Fancy word for a mirror.

Cycle lane: Footpath.

Stop sign: No such thing.

Hand signal: Something deaf people use.

Bell: A yoke in a church steeple.

Pedestrian: A target.

High-vis clothing: A T-shirt that reads 'Beans Meanz Fartz.'

Helmet: A German boy's name?

Drunk cycling: A means of sobering up after the pub.

One-way street: Two-way street.

Motorist: The Prince of Darkness.

What cyclists really want.

52 Misuse of the Word 'Bonus'

There has been much discussion on the bonus culture that has infected our country for the last couple of decades and judging by relatively recent revelations by certain skivers in various charities, banks, public service departments, hospitals and public utilities, it is still as common as a slapper's make-up.

But that debate is dealt with elsewhere. This section merely seeks to deal with the grammatical aspect of the subject, i.e. the frequent misuse of 'bonus' by assorted politicians, journalists and self-serving scumbags, who like to give themselves and their buddies loads of free dosh.

According to the *Oxford English Dictionary*, a bonus is 'a sum of money added to a person's wage for good performance.'

The *Collins Dictionary* has a similar interpretation: 'Something given, paid, or received, above what is due or expected.'

Clearly the term is being widely misapplied in Ireland and a campaign is obviously needed to reclaim the word 'bonus' for those deserving of one. As a means of initiating this, here is a selection of scenarios featuring alternative words/terms that more accurately describe the extra payments made to financial chiefs, heads of companies, senior public servants, members of the boards of certain charities, and so on.

'Senior managers at Irish Water are in line for a ~~bonus~~ **backhander** of 9% even if they get an assessment rating that says they need improvement.'

'It emerged late last year that one senior Bank of Ireland executive was paid a reported €500,000 in one ~~bonus~~ **sack of free loot for being incompetent** last year.'

'The CEO of the charity said that the board ~~taking bonuses~~ **diddling huge wads of dosh** from people's donations was completely ethical.'

'The union spokesman was quoted as saying that senior public servants are fully entitled to ~~their bonuses~~ **rip-off ginormous amounts of taxpayer's money for doing feck all.**'

Hopefully these few suggestions will get the ball rolling, and future commentary on the issue will apply more appropriate terminology. If only for the sake of the English language.

53 BEING PESTERED AND RECORDED BY TELEPHONE MARKETING COMPANIES

You know how it goes – some annoying gobshite rings you to try and convince you to switch your broadband company or something, and they always start with the line 'we are recording this conversation for training purposes', or some such utter claptrap.

First off, you don't have to keep being pestered by these eejits. Get in contact with your telephone service provider and tell them you don't want any more unsolicited calls. Go ahead! Do it now! It will really piss them off and save you hours of irritating conversations with people trying to get their hands on your money. Once you call Eircom, BT, Vodafone or whoever, according to Data Protection legislation your name and number will be marked as 'opted out' on the National Directory Database and it will be illegal for the feckers to ring you. For some unfathomable reason, this takes them a month to achieve. How in shite's name can it take a month to tap a few keys on a computer?

Anyway, while you're waiting for the sleeveens to opt you out, you will probably still be pestered. Which brings

us to the annoying matter of recording your conversations. Unfortunately, because our legislators are as useless as a carpet-fitter's ladder it is perfectly legal for a company to record a conversation with only one party's consent. However, that doesn't mean you have to agree to it. So the next time some irritating sales gobdaw rings you and starts with the line 'I'm obliged to tell you that this conversation is being recorded for training purposes', tell him/her that you object to being recorded. This will totally bamboozle the poor eejit who will then start to splutter and stammer and say it is out of his or her control, at which point you tell him/her that that's their problem and hang up.

A fun alternative is to inform the guy that, if they are recording you, you are also making your own recording. This invariably causes consternation – the poor sales pest suddenly feels like his/her privacy is being violated, or that there is some sinister motive behind your behaviour and they will often object or become completely flustered, at which point you, chuckling to yourself, can refuse to continue the conversation unless they give you permission to record the call, or hang up.

As regards calls from abroad, particularly the ones claiming to be calling from 'the Microsoft computer department', two sharply delivered words will bring the conversation to an abrupt end. One starts with 'f' and ends with 'k' and the other is 'off'.

Honestly, there are no ends of fun you can have annoying the annoying phone marketers!

Good day, sir. I would like to tell you of a great way to get rid of unsolicited calls...

54 THE INSURANCE RACKET

No, this is not about the bowsies who pretend they've gotten whiplash after someone taps their rear bumper or the lowlifes who stage fake accidents and claim thousands. This is about the racket perpetrated by Irish insurance companies whose premiums are based, not on any calculation of prices versus payouts, but are set by working out the minimum they need to charge to make a profit and then simply plucking a figure miles above that out of thin air.

But it's not, they'll claim with outrage! The cost of insurance premiums is based on long-established methodology, they'll scream. But if they all use the same methodology then why are there such huge variations between a) different Irish companies, and b) everywhere else on the planet? The answer is simple – insurance is something you usually have to have, certainly in terms of car insurance – it is not a luxury item you can choose to buy or not buy. In other words the geebags have you by the short and curlies and they use that position to screw every cent they can out of you. In short, they are a bunch of money-grabbing, greedy gougers.

Unfortunately, in Ireland, we're a lazy lot, which fact helps

143

to line the insurers' pockets even more. You see, when it comes to renewal time, a lot of companies simply hike up their premiums. They know that many people will continue to pay the increased premium through a standing order without noticing the price hike, or else they won't take the time to ring up and find out why their bill has suddenly increased by bleedin' 50%. If people did keep an eye on their insurance premiums, they'd quickly realise how much they're being scammed.

Repeated surveys show that shopping around for say, car insurance, can save people hundreds, if not thousands of euro. It's the same with home insurance and travel insurance and all other types of insurance – insurance chicanery is rampant. So do your bit – shop around, save yourself a packet and get on the shitehawks' tits at the same time.

In fact, make it your number one policy.

INSURE-A-PET

The astronomical cost is due to the nine lives thing.